'The step in the presence of the Lion,
towards the Lion,
is a great and rare matter.
This is the true step in a human life,
the rest are mere footprints.'

Rumi

Dear brother Niall,
 well — my humble effort to tell
 a story about answering an
 inner call — as well as some
 of my other, more foolish
 adventures. Hoping There is
 something in it of interest
 for you.

with Love always

Greg 'Arjuna' Govinda

2.12.2015

Towards the Lion
Govinda, Arjuna, 1956-

Deva Wings Publications 2015

Copyright (c) G. A. Govindamurti 2015

Deva Wings Publications
www.devawings.com
Daylesford, Australia

National Library of Australia Cataloguing-in-Publication entry:
Govinda, Arjuna, author.
Towards the lion / Arjuna Govinda.
ISBN: 9780958720205 (paperback)
Govinda, Arjuna.
Spiritual life.
Spiritual healing.
Mind and body.
Self-realization.

294.3444

Deva Wings Publications

Daylesford, Australia
www.devawings.com

With eternal gratitude to my beloved parents

For all who seek Love and Truth

Index

Please note:

I sometimes capitalise words to denote a divine aspect of that quality. For example, 'love' as human, and 'Love' as divine.

Prologue

This book has been written to share something of my journey to wholeness over the past forty years, as I searched for love, understanding, and connection with peace. It reflects on times of passion and ignorance, frustration and freedom, tests and trials, adventures, and eventually finding meaning and purpose in life. It is a story about the choices I made, as I sought to understand the human condition. I wanted to know why people didn't treat each other better, and how I might help this to change.

The book offers my recollections of walking a spiritual path and the basics of becoming a better person: the lessons I had to learn; the karma that needed paying, and the challenges of an expanding consciousness. Ultimately, it seems to be about learning to love and accept myself, and to trust life as it is. The journey necessarily took a lot of effort, but when my spirit called, I was happy to answer. And when lost at various times, angels guided me.

In contemplating the journey as a whole, an image presents itself: the forging of a sword. The raw material is heated, purified and then bashed into shape, until eventually it is refined to its intended form. The sword is then sharpened and readied for service. A similar process is encountered by one who aspires to be a knight.

Now, worn down by life's processes, I follow my heart, in the hope that my life might be of service. There is nothing fanatical in this but merely the hope to bring more love and joy, caring and respect into a needy world; finally, to stand in awe, share the joys, and appreciate how beautiful life is.

I hope that my journey inspires something in you, for yours.

~ Arjuna

01 - An Embattled Past

'I am the clash of opposites.'
(C. G. Jung)

At the age of seventeen, I was already in need of an epiphany. Secondary school was wearing and I took to mixing alcohol with my lunch-box cordial. Seeking 'spirit' to lift me from the restrictions of youth and social mores, I thought I could get it from a bottle. Clearly, there were many problems I would need to face to get through this period, and many rough edges that would need to be smoothed out. I was frustrated in my pursuit of love and pleasure, and I had much to learn about pretty much everything. For whatever reasons, I was oblivious of how to care for myself and others, and I fought against the environments I found myself in. There were rebellious energies within me, and it would take many years for me to learn to relax, and be at peace in this world.

I had the idea of becoming a carpenter but my destiny sent me to college instead. I struggled in many of the classes, which was probably something that brought out the rebel in me. I took issue with people using the guise of authority to dominate me, and this ensured that I was beaten daily. These punishments were sometimes dished out by student bullies, offended by my being forthright, but most often by those who called themselves Christian Brothers. The Brothers were men who had dedicated themselves to religious life and the vocation of teaching. Unfortunately for me and the other children, as part of their teaching methods, some of the Brothers inflicted regular physical pain and psychological torment on their students. In younger years we were subject to being strapped for every wrong answer given, starting most days with at least two lashes. This was never okay with me. It was bad enough that they belittled me, making me wear short pants and a school cap, and having my hair cut to a style of their choosing. Being strapped daily was incredibly painful and the only relief was to get back to my seat as quickly as possible, and wrap the stinging fingers and palms around the cold steel frame of the classroom desk. In a way, this was just a continuation of the harm that had been inflicted on us by some of the nuns in primary school. There, they used timber rulers, which sometimes included metal edges, as they struck down across the wrists or against the palms. I was used to it, but not happy about it.

Though interested in academic subjects, I found myself drawn mostly to art, poetry, and philosophy. In class, we were expected to memorise wads of irrelevant facts, and this was neither engaging, nor within my capabilities. Some of the subjects held my interest but the school wielded the constant threat of, 'Do what we tell you, or be beaten', which brought out a natural rebellion in me. I couldn't help but taunt these people who wanted to subdue my spirit with their menacing threats and violent acts.

The best part about school was making lifetime friends with some very dear people. We had many things in common but what became the main focus at school was our interest in gambling and playing cards. The other guys seemed to thrive on understanding the odds, while I just enjoyed the dynamics of random play. We would also take time out from our classes to go to someone's house to watch major racing and boxing events. I wasn't interested in horses or boxing but I relished my friends company and the excitement they had in such activities.

Out of school times, I took refuge in spending time alone, listening to music and walking the streets at night with my dog. I was uplifted by Beethoven and the Beatles, as well as the hippy philosophies of the late 1960's. I found eastern wisdom through practicing yoga, and I developed my political ideas through my beloved Dad. George Orwell, Voltaire, Oscar Wilde and George Bernard Shaw were some of my early teachers. I also looked to the visionaries in Buddha, Jesus, Gandhi, Mother Teresa and Martin Luther King Jr. Physics and chemistry were interesting enough but my mind was more drawn to eastern philosophy, and the ideas of popular musicians like Cat Stevens, Melanie Safka and John Lennon. I also began to be influenced by the worlds of Elton John, Joe Cocker, The Moody Blues and Janis Joplin. In the music, I found an aspiration that matched my Aquarian dreaming. I was an idealist and mystic, interested in the esoteric, negotiating with a society that placed most of its belief in materialism and the physical-mental realm.

In being educated in a Catholic institution, I suffered many challenges to my own insights, but there were several aspects that I can be honestly grateful for. One was the priest, in whom I found a positive role model. I didn't know him that well but just enjoyed his general demeanour. Another gift was having a chapel that I could retreat to and sit quietly amidst the general business of the school day. I loved the peace that was present in the chapel. The place was considered sacrosanct and it was perfect to just sit or lie down on a pew and go within for half an hour. The chapel provided a place of profound peace relative to the rest of the school. A third thing that I am grateful for is that, despite the violence perpetrated against me in the initial years, I was introduced to the concept of a Divine Source; the matter of One Life; the idea of 'God.' I am not grateful for the constant torment imposed upon me by being denied my own enquiries, but in that I was given an introduction to the mere possibility of such a thing at an early age. This supported me in seeking life beyond the limited rational level, which would be a significant enquiry throughout my life.

At school I had taken the best from what was on offer, but in Teachers College I was finally free to choose my own path. Institutionalised and unsure of what to do in life, I followed the path that school had furrowed. I enrolled in topics of interest that included politics, sociology and literature. As my first venture into doing something that I actually wanted to do, I made my way to the table where they offered Media Studies. This included photography, which was something I had enjoyed for most of my life. The tutor, Terry, was a delightful man in whose smile I met a kindred spirit. I took the risk to do something that was in my heart and began my new life.

Apart from the wonder I experienced in photography and cinema classes, the rest of the place didn't touch my heart at all. I struggled with my studies for nearly a year, until I noticed how bright eyed and playful the students of drama and theatre studies were. There was something in this that attracted me strongly, and I was willing to face many fears to enter that world. Drama taught me to explore the depths of feelings, share private thoughts, and speak out about issues that felt important to me. It gave me an outlet to be spectacularly alive.

With my dear Mum's support I purchased a 550cc motorbike, and before very long was enthralled with speed. There was something about the bike that resonated with my need to feel free. I named it Ganga, and found what felt like love for this precious machine. I knew that it wasn't true love, but it was certainly a kind of love for me. My heart was enamoured by the thing itself, and by what it could do. I was now able to travel at high speeds and experience passion and an emotional and mental ecstasy. The bike awakened me to a sense of power and adventure that had been unavailable to me for too many years.

My grandmother warned me that I was burning the candle at both ends, but my naively blind reply was, 'Yes, and in the middle as well!' My grandfather also tried to warn me by relating the story of Toad from *Wind in the Willows*, but I was far too gone for that. I was too young to know the consequences of my brash way of thinking, but I would soon find out.

Feeling Alive

Going fast on my motorbike became a major focus at that time. The more risks I took, the more I felt alive. My character was changing and I became less concerned about boundaries or good behavior much of the time. Riding was releasing much of my suppressed passions all at once. I took the dangers seriously enough, and trained myself at being able to manage at high speeds as well as ride close to the ground when cornering. Too often the foot peg caught in the bitumen and I was thrown off. I practiced regularly on a rough road that I knew to have unexpected dangers, and pushed myself at negotiating these. Often there was discarded rubbish that would have thrown the bike completely, and I enjoyed riding hard and avoiding these. I played with speed and power as well as developing my abilities. The play was certainly exciting but was also taking me away from being sensitive, to myself as well as others. On one occasion I miscalculated and nearly ended up underneath a tram. On another, I skidded at least seven metres on my back after I had come off the bike. I was very pleasantly surprised to be upright and okay at the end of that. The leathers saved me from any serious injuries on several occasions. On the open road in top gear, I loved to lie horizontal on the bike. It was the closest thing I experienced to flying. The problem was that when I hit a bump in the road for some time I was actually airborne, separate from the machine. Many of my pursuits were too foolish to relate in detail here. I'm just grateful to have survived.

At college I studied four subjects at a time, and drama alone took at least forty hours each week. Thursday through Saturday I did paid work in the theatre at night, and any time I had left needed to cover the other three subjects. It was a very hectic schedule for many years, but one that I thoroughly enjoyed. One of my other subjects was dance, and this at least kept me fit. With a clear sense of body and self, I feasted on such a rich life.

When possible, I would complete six weeks study in five and then take a week off. As well as the motorbike, I had a station wagon and would spend the week with my dog, camping by the side of a river. To balance out such a hectic agenda, I loved doing nothing for a time. Living simply by a quiet river was pure peace. Australia was the perfect place for a wanderer and nature dweller in the mid 1970's.

In drama, both in the classroom and on stage we explored many aspects of human nature. The course was intensely engaging and allowed me to learn a lot about the human spirit, as well as who I was personally. It enabled a deep exploration of my mental, physical and emotional cores. It is where I first opened to Shakespeare's idea that 'All the world's a stage / and all the men and women merely players'. There were so many ways to view the world and here was an opportunity to explore many of them. I was filled with ideas of a better world and I broadcast my opinions openly. I also challenged anyone I met in whom I sensed a blinkered view of things. If someone believed in limitation, I felt the need to argue with them about that. Often I began conversations with strangers in hotel bars, making contentious statements. I narrowly missed taking many beatings but usually made new friends by the end of these purposeful confrontations. I felt a need to challenge my society to include broader views. I found it difficult to relax within the pressures and suffering created by a narrow-minded status quo.

After nearly a decade of repressing my sexuality, I finally met my first lover, Alexandria. Most of my adolescence had been frustrated by the Catholic imposition of 'no sex before marriage' and this, I believed at the time, had been a large influence on subverting my energies. Not only did it hinder me from being at peace in the world, it pushed me to chase stimulant-induced states, and to engage in danger and excitement as compensations. I am in fact, very grateful and fortunate to still be alive.

My lover was twice my age and quite flighty. We enjoyed some lovely times together but we also had difficulties in maintaining a stable relationship. Alex never seemed at peace and this was possibly because she tried to deny and hide her age from me. At one point I thought she was pregnant and was excited at the idea of becoming a father. Alex had a different view, horrified at the idea and relieved that nothing came of it. Eventually we went our own ways and I found myself seeking sex with many other partners. My ego was involved, and I would need to learn to distinguish love from desire.

At 21, I had little sensitivity to others feelings in my pursuit for experiencing pleasure. It would take some time for me to come to my senses again and be able to enjoy just being with women for who they were. I believed that I had missed out on a natural progression of sensuality in adolescence, and now that I could finally begin to enjoy intimacy, I held nothing back. Suppression had created discordance, and it would take time and effort to raise and purify these vibrations.

For years, part of me had yearned to live in a utopian state, such as I imagined some islander life might have been in earlier times. I found it almost impossible to understand why my society valued materialism over community wellbeing and intimacy. I took to heart Cat Stevens song, 'Where Do The Children Play?' I was deeply concerned that the world was covering everything in concrete, bitumen and buildings and too little value placed on providing safe and natural places for the children to enjoy. Later I would see how the circumstances of my life were the result of excessive indulgences in previous lifetimes. I needed to repay and balance my karma, learning to find respect and caring in relationships.

For a time I was free flowing, out of balance and indulging in pleasure for pleasure's sake. I became sexually active and ignored most of the rules that I had been raised to believe in. I needed to explore life for myself, and get to know what was within my own heart. Some of my choices led to me being homeless for a time, and this was a wound that would take many years to heal. At least now I can feel some assurance that I not only grew out of those times, but because of them. It would take meeting Amrita to bring me back to the fun and ease of loving-kindness. I called Amrita 'China' because of her fine qualities and because I found her as interesting and complex as the culture of that great country. I delighted in her bright and cheerful nature. She had a natural love of life and she was very good for me. We became the best of friends and I loved sharing relaxed times with her. My heart lifted whenever I saw her. I felt a natural high and delight in her company. She had the most inspiring laugh and sense of joy about her. I was very taken by the beauty of her smile and so grateful that she enjoyed my company as well.

China worked as secretary for the drama department so I got to see her during the day sometimes, as well as on weekends. She was a wonderful and supportive friend and lover, and we enjoyed many fun times together. Finally, I had a relationship where I could express my whole self and enjoy the beauty of being close to someone very special to me. China shared an apartment with a girlfriend and I was able to visit and stay over at any time. This gave me a deep sense of freedom and welcome that I needed. The time with Amrita made the last years of my college studies not just bearable but enjoyable.

Apart from the support of Amrita's dear company, I was challenged by having to attend teaching rounds. The school environments felt quite hostile and I often found myself at the receiving end of people's anger. Something as simple as drinking from another teacher's coffee cup could set people off for weeks. There was a great deal of chaos in the schools I attended, and I often had to break up fights between young boys. Vandalism was prevalent and regular, and there was a strong element of frustration and acting-out amongst the children. It seemed unreasonable to put children in such an unnatural environment and then expect them to blossom. More than a few times, I imbibed a bottle of tequila the night before a teaching round, in order to justify calling in sick.

I was soon to graduate from College and enter the school system again, as a full-time teacher. I applied to my old secondary school but received a rejection letter. It was only then that I became aware of my fury at that institution. I had put up with so many beatings, mental belittling and other harassments during my junior and high school years. I saw a vision of myself as Samson at the pillars, tearing the school down to its very foundations. It was for the good-of-all that they had declined my application.

While Teachers College had trained us to be creative and enthusiastic about life, I was assigned to work at a school holding an older, control-oriented paradigm. What they professed to stand for and what they actually delivered were quite contrasting. What ensued between the school and myself was the meeting of two distinct fronts, like one sees in a weather map, where different pressure zones are the makings of a storm.

It was exciting starting at work. I had been at Teachers College for five years, and now was the opportunity to share what I had learned. I was only 22 years old, and had enormous energy for my tasks. In the first two weeks I introduced myself to the other teachers and learned the names of a few hundred children. Not having any immediate classes gave me the chance to meet people but it was also disorienting. I was given a desk but nowhere to put my things. I stored my bike helmet and jacket on the floor under my desk and made a bookshelf out of bricks and boards for my folders and books. It was more rudimentary than what the other teachers had but at least I had a space to call my own. My desk was positioned in the doorway so that student enquiries met me first. I liked to think I had been put there because of my enthusiasm but in fact I had merely filled the last available space in a crowded office. At least I was inside the door and not in the hallway itself. There would soon be another addition to the humanities staff, and longer-serving staff members expressed strong negativity about it. They seemed fearful of losing some of their workload and I only hoped that this didn't also apply to me. There were a dozen teachers sharing the same space and I was quite aware of the variety of energies that were flying around. The teachers were quite forthright in expressing their feelings and perhaps they were not aware of the intense affect this had on others. Working with children six hours a day put most of them under a lot of pressure.

The head of department was very kind and invited me to his place for dinner. I felt very welcomed by him and his family. I was vegetarian at the time and this was quite rare in those days. We had a roast dinner and the children delighted in informing me that they were eating their pet sheep Gough. We were clearly from different worlds but I could appreciate their love and generosity.

All new staff members were invited to the principal's house for an evening. I already felt a little like a fish out of water in this foreign place, but this particular evening made it clear that the principal and I would never see eye to eye. Rad related how he categorised the various kinds of teachers, and he looked directly at me when he spoke of the 'avant-garde.' I probably could have taken this as a compliment, but it seemed that he was stating that I just wouldn't fit in. From that moment on, we each found it near impossible to work together. I felt judged by him, and I also judged him as being authoritarian and for having misunderstood me.

One of my first tasks was when the ten senior staff of the Human Relations course asked me if I would be the coordinator. I felt honoured by their belief in me, but they also asked that I convey to the principal, on their behalf, that they didn't want him in the program anymore. The H-R course was about helping the students prepare themselves for the wider world, and the staff felt it was inappropriate for the principal to be involved.

I approached Rad about the two issues as diplomatically as I could, but he dismissed both propositions on the spot. Already I had been placed between two factions in the school, and would need to continue to negotiate that.

Early Pressures

Pressures began almost immediately. One of the Form 5 girls threatened that if I didn't have sex with her, she would inform the local community that I had. Sexual advances from some of the other female students were also very confronting. As a 22 year-old male I had to establish boundaries very clearly. Other teachers informed me to be very careful to never be alone in a room with only one student. There was a great deal to learn and I had to learn it as soon as possible.

Rad decided that he wasn't keen on my image, which including my riding a motorbike. He didn't like my haircut, choice of shoes, or that I wore an earning. Each time we had one of his little chats, he would share something else about me that he wasn't comfortable with. There was at least one of these talks each week and it began to get on my nerves. I didn't like anyone trying to reduce me to something I was not, so I responded by expanding my freedom of expression.

It seemed to me that the organisation didn't respect individual uniqueness or value peace. Everything was pressured, with chaos in between. The school's charter declared high aims for how students would be treated, but this seemed purely theoretical. Many old attitudes were embedded in the practices. The agendas I was expected to follow were not my own and, as much as I respected the people within the system, I could not surrender my desire to see change.

School life reminded me of the story of a village whose citizens had drunk from a poisoned well and gone mad. I was like those few who had abstained and were seen as the crazy ones. I considered my options, one being to drink from the common well. I chose to resist.

Within a few months of the start of the year, an issue arose where our Union asked members to come to a fellow teacher's aid. This lead to many months of intermittent work. The government dug in and the teachers involved increased strike action. Soon we only came to work on Mondays and Fridays so that we wouldn't lose all of our pay. The strike action went on for several months and created many deep divisions within the school. Many went on strike while some continued to work. This became an open wound that would take years to heal. It was to be a significant event contributing to the disharmony within the school and between different groups of staff.

Being on staff meant having to attend meetings at the end of many days. Meetings would often last for at least two hours, repeatedly examining pedantic matters. At the conclusion of the evenings we were asked for our final opinions. My contribution would often be the simple question: 'Why aren't we at the beach watching the sun go down?'

Many thought I wasn't taking the meetings seriously. I was involved in my own way. I was less engaged by talking about problems and more interested in being fully alive.

Moments Lost

When I wasn't working, I enjoyed living a half hour ride away. I shared a house in a picturesque seaside town, with the waters of Bass Strait not far from my door. On my days off I lived in paradise. The township was undeveloped at the time and the locals loved living there. We still had many dirt roads and the Australian bush was intact. I now had a Mini-Moke and just left the keys under the car seat when I wasn't using it. I also never locked the back door of my home. The township felt safe and very relaxed about such matters. It was quiet and peaceful, and I enjoyed living in such an easygoing community.

China and I would take turns visiting each other, depending on how busy a week either of us had worked. We got to see each other regularly but I could feel a pull within me to stay in the countryside more often. A fellow teacher had a weekend party at her place in the country and China and I set up tent for the weekend. Within minutes it was very obvious that my beloved partner was a city girl, and took no joy whatsoever in living anywhere near the land. My life was now committed to work in the country and China knew that she would never be able to enjoy life there. Quite sadly we knew that we had to go our separate ways.

I was fortunate to soon make friends with a fellow teacher, Bruce, who had also just parted from his wife. We often shared our philosophies on life and loss late into the night, with the support of whiskey and bottles of red wine. For a period we found that intense partying helped to quell our hearts' pain. We lived hard and it felt like good release from some of the pressures at work. Under the influence of grief and alcohol, our war cry became 'run away!' Whenever we were challenged at work, one of us would just yell that, and we would make a tactical retreat. Our out-of-work habits diminished some of our previously professional engagement. It was like becoming an unchecked teenager again. We were too often drunk and regressing.

Bruce lent me all his rock 'n' roll albums and these became our theme music for the time. In those days, my naivety with emotional issues was a wild ingredient in everything I did. The wisdom I wanted was going to be hard won.

Rad, the principal, kept up his insistence that the community didn't understand me, and voiced his concerns that parents would see me as too far outside the norm. He continued his little talks with me about how I looked and I continued to push back against this. I was getting tired of his constant projections and, when attending a party, I shaved my head in Mohican style as part of my costume. I shaved my head clean before going back to work the next day, but in 1979 this wasn't common, or very well received. Rad wanted me to conform, and I insisted on my right to be who I was. I also had no idea how to allay his fears or satisfy his wants, even if I would have tried. I couldn't comprehend how to live my life by what somebody else might want of me.

I was a drama teacher and, to me, that was about experiential learning. Accordingly, I often wore clothing as costume. In this way I could engage the students in creative explorations. By coincidence or design, I had dressed up as a soldier the day that the army recruitment officer was coming to the school. I wanted the students to think for themselves, so I made discipline the theme of the day. In classes, I barked my orders and gave the students the experience of being on the receiving end of them. This probably offended some of the other teachers, as I was soon called to the principal's office yet again.

The pressures continued to build and I was still drinking more than was good for me. I was losing my grounding and also using the bike inappropriately. I was holding to the theory that 'death is a lie' and I went to the very edges of life without fear. The more I drank, the more I risks I took. I could tell that I was beginning to lose the plot and disengage from the career that I had trained for. At a party I noticed a woman I was attracted to and asked her if she would go around Australia with me. I desired a life more fulfilling than the one I was caught in and I told her I was happy to leave my job the next day and travel with her. I knew nothing about her and it was an absurd proposal. She turned me down, which was probably a wise decision on her part!

Eventually things settled down a bit. Bruce and I went our own ways. We were still close friends but he had met his future wife. Pressures at work were no easier, except for the arrival of a student-teacher who caught my eye. At first sight, I knew I had met my complement. I felt what I thought was a spiritual connection with her, and followed her home one evening. Her name was Angie and I thought she was my lady-for-life.

As the work year neared its end, I was worn out. I moved house to an hour north of where I worked, dropping everything to move in with my new love. There were four of us in the house, three art students and me. It made for a lot of fun, and a fantastic break from the pressures of work. The mornings were hectic as we each raced off to our daily grinds. One Hall and Oates album was played repeatedly, complimenting the feelings of love and joy that were rising in me. On my hour drive to school I would listen to Bob Marley, and charge myself up to get through the work day and complete an exhausting year.

Angie and I were lovers, but perhaps more by accident than stars aligning. It was an unconscious union. I felt such deep attraction for her, but nothing seemed to gel. She often met my enthusiasm for life with a disinclination to join in. We did things together but weren't yet finding a place of mutual peace. Something was troubling Angie deeply and she seemed vulnerable to depression. Perhaps I was ignoring the fact that we had little in common, or perhaps I just wasn't sensitive enough to know what she was going through. I was very attracted to Angie, despite our inability to find or create joy. I also began to feel children wanting to be born through me. There was a very clear energy in which I could feel that these souls wanted to incarnate. I sensed a light in the sky that wanted to descend and enter the world through me. Angie didn't want anything to do with having children, while I felt almost divinely moved. It felt like twins.

Angie became pregnant and wasn't happy about it at all. Bruce drove over to where we were living and helped me to take her to the hospital for a check. She was with the doctor for some time and when she came out she was quite distressed. We drove home and later Angie told me she had miscarried. It wasn't until many years later that I wondered if she had organised an abortion, and just not told me about it. Angie seemed more depressed than usual and I felt very flat about the fact that she didn't want children with me, or feel able to come out of her grief. We had only known each for some months, so having children was probably quite impractical timing anyway. At 22 years of age I just wanted to experience the fullness of life.

By now I was mentally tired, and one morning it showed. I went to leave for work and my car became surrounded by a large herd of cows. We were staying in an old farmhouse and these fascinating creatures, in their inquisitiveness, pushed my car down the hill into deep mud. I was already late and used to being browbeaten for endless things. That day, whatever came over me, I lay in the field and just admired the light and the nature. I was aware that work would be furious but I had no phone. I simply told a passing crow to please pass on to work that I wouldn't be in that day and enjoyed my day off in the countryside.

The next day I went to the vice-principal to apologise and he wasn't impressed. I insisted that he give me a break, as I already knew I was in trouble. When I got a free hour I went for a ride on my motorbike to try and burn away the stress within me from working in such a system. I was surprisingly well protected in surviving these steam-releasing rides. My guardian angel must have been working a lot of overtime in keeping me alive.

That day I came across a general store that was selling gladioli flowers, and purchased the lot. Heading back to school I stood at the central corridor with armfuls of flowers, and handed them out to students and staff, with love. I was happy at the joy the flowers gave to people, and watched how the love radiated out into the whole school. It was a kind of revolutionary act, to give love, when the organisation seemed to demand excess controls and stress. I had put up with enough, of the system trying to impose itself upon me, and gave myself over to the love instead.

The Coming Storm

The pressures at work added to strains in my home life, and visa versa. In all it was quite a crazy year. In the holidays, Angie and I realised that we had little in common except for our hopes of love. We moved to the city for the summer, and then back again to the country in the new year.

I began the second year of my teaching work with full enthusiasm, even though it had taken me all of the summer holidays to muster. First day back the mood amongst the other teachers was already quite grim. The head art teacher spoke often of how one day he would leave. Others informed me he had been saying this for the past decade. He had such a beautiful heart, and was one of the people who brought humour and joy to the place. He was such a radiant light, but his heart was being slowly crushed by not living his dreams. My own dreams were taking quite a battering as well. I fully believed in education as the way to advance our society, but was fast wondering if this was possible in a state school environment.

The school had been having discussions on what to make its official school uniform. Most argued for 'girls in checked dresses, and boys in long pants.' My offering, that I thought just as worthy of consideration, was 'everyone in pink overhauls.' My contribution didn't go down well, and as usual the other staff didn't take me seriously. I liked to think laterally, and I always offered my best, but it was as if I was the only one who contemplated colour, in a world that preferred to remain grey.

On arrival at work I was told that they had cancelled all my classes for the day. I was to attend a meeting at department headquarters and take instruction. In the meeting I was told that they preferred that I discontinued wearing overhauls to work. I had somehow crossed a line in wearing a costume that did not fit how they perceived my role. As a drama teacher they wanted me to dress accordingly. To the authorities, a drama teacher would wear neat casual, with or without a tie. It was preferred that I did not wear overhauls, as I was not a technical studies teacher. I often wondered what differences there were between those days in 1980 and medieval times. There were still so many ways in which our consciousness was stuck in the past. I was Aquarian, with an Aquarian mind, perhaps trying to live fifty years ahead of most of my peers. Now I can see the value of so many different perceptions, but in those days, I mostly experienced a world that wanted me to be the one to change.

I had driven an hour to get to work, and a further hour to this meeting. I was expected to return the hour back to work before heading, yet another hour back home. Back at work Rad called me into his office. Again he pushed his case. My dilemma was how I could surrender to acting normal, if my very job was to assist others to explore their uniqueness and creativity. I saw it as my work, to help others to question and awaken to their true selves. Perhaps I was full of youthful arrogance or ignorance, but at the time I saw it as fighting for my freedom to be. With so many forces trying to extinguish me, I felt my resistance was a holy quest. A quest for wholeness.

That night on the way home, I passed a shop where I saw a pair of large Dutch clogs in the window. To my delight they were my size, and they were for sale. I purchased the clogs, painted them

22

a brilliant gloss enamel red, and wore them to work the next day. They made quite a loud noise on the linoleum hallways, and it felt good to express my right to exist. I also replaced the small silver earning that I wore in my left ear, with a large seagull feather that I had found on the beach. The centimetre long earring, which Rad objected to, was now replaced by one that was 25 centimetres long. Rad's objections to how I expressed myself brought out a very spirited and determined warrior in me.

When the children confided in me how the teachers were beating them, I just laughed. When I noticed the horror on their faces, I realised they were telling me the truth. One of the staff members had been going through marital difficulties, and taking out his pain on the children. He would chalk noughts and crosses on the end of a one metre wooden ruler, and then beat the children until the chalk was rubbed off. Only five of us out of more than 100 staff, were concerned enough to address the issue. Our small group managed to have the beatings stopped, but alienated many of the other teachers. This was a country school in 1980.

I put a note across my work desk that read: 'Lost in a world that is more lost than I am.' There was no professional counselling available for teachers at that time, and no one questioned me as to how I was. I also added a phrase by Oscar Wilde: 'Education is a wonderful thing, but it is worth noting from time to time; that nothing that is worth knowing, can be taught.' In a room of a dozen staff, no one questioned me about this either.

I painted my Mini-Moke pink and put its name on the bonnet. I named it *Euphonious Whale* for the image it invoked in me of a beautiful creature that sang to life. The state of the car seemed to express my declining health. The spare wheel fell off one day without my knowing and the canvas roof tore open. Every time I drove to work in the rain I was drenched by the time I arrived. The rear view mirror fell off and the car needed to be push-started every morning. I lived on mostly flat ground, so I had to push it the length of the street before I got to a hill steep enough to get the car going. This was quite an exhausting and inconvenient way of getting to work each day. When the car continued having mechanical issues I painted it brilliant red. This seemed to help, so I also painted many other things I owned. I knew it made no sense whatsoever, but it did seem to work. Perhaps it just stimulated me to be more alert and not worry as much.

The pressures just kept building and the alienation increased. I managed to move from the humanities department to the art teachers' portable where I found many kind-hearted people. The art teachers' portable was away from the main body of the school and this helped as well, except in that I had to run long distances to get to my various classes and meetings, but I was much happier there amongst my own kind.

I spent all the money I could make or borrow to support Angie and I, although she left me in the house by myself during the week, only visiting on the weekends. She bought a German Shepherd pup and left it with me to look after, which complicated my life. This dear dog would eat through whatever fencing I put up. One day he even ate through rabbit wire. I was met at the door one night by a neighbor threatening to shoot the dog if he got out one more time.

When Angie finally got a job after six months or more, she didn't want to help me in paying the rent or other costs. She wanted to have her own money for a while. This left me broke and in debt, and as the only provider. We each struggled in working out what we wanted in life. There was no lack of kindness, just two young souls trying to work out relationship and care of self.

I felt abandoned and descended into watching Jean-Luc Godard movies at home on my own. I had access to various embassy archives on 16 mm, and spent my evenings in a world film festival for one. These were not happy times but I enjoyed the stimulation of obscure art. I read *Zorba the Greek* and began to consider Kazantzakis idea as a serious option: That 'a man needs a little madness, or else he never dares cut the rope and be free.'

I knew that I was losing the plot when I attended a party dressed as a fried egg. My creativity was flowing and I had made the costume by painting a large yellow yolk on a white bed sheet. Everyone else at the party was in semi-formal wear while I was wearing nothing but a sheet. I was beginning to think that I was a little far-gone, on my road less travelled.

Go Mad Now

I can't recall where I met him but Don was a delightful and gentle man. He had been a window dresser for a department store and recently retired as a psychiatric nurse. He was a wonderful character who enjoyed attending auction rooms in his spare time. I took an immediate liking to his bright view of life. He often gathered people around him and we enjoyed many quiet afternoons together. Being with Don and his friends was such a relaxing thing to do. Don entertained us with his loving humour, and we enjoyed general play and celebration of life. We also supped tea.

When I shared with Don about the stress I was under, his advice was 'go mad now; before you break dear boy.' I must have been near the end of my wits, as I went around work telling people that I was going to go mad. Little did I know how close I was to the brink.

I began to contemplate how I could become of more value to the world. As an educator, I was far too disappointed and disillusioned with the school system. I wondered if I would have been of more use as a busker or clown. I felt that any real education within the education system was near impossible.

A travelling theatre group came to perform for the teaching staff one night. The liveliest of the characters spoke about a fool who thought he could 'change the system from within.' This comment struck such a deep chord in me that without any forethought I asked one of the Art teachers if I could move in with him. I would leave my relationship with Angie the following week.

I was fed up trying to get close to Angie; it had been a mismatch. I offered her joy but she stuck with her fears. I gave her support and she moved away. My love for her was quite likely an unconscious projection but when we parted, I felt like I had been torn open, right down the middle. The entire front of my body felt like it was ripped away. The only way I was able to lessen the intense pain, was to curl over and try to seal the wound. This meant withdrawing from being able to feel and this numbness remained with me for many years.

In my desire for intimacy and closeness, I had attracted someone who was in great emotional pain. I gave Angie everything I was able but I ended up hurting myself. We were both young and inexperienced in matters of the heart. Most of what I knew about relationships were ideals and aspirations that I received from watching movies, or platitudes I had taken on board as an impressionable child. I gave Angie one year of my life and it took me ten to recover from losing her. I wanted her to be my lady-for-life but this was more of a projected idea than an honest appraisal of our potential.

By September I was at my wits' end. My boundaries were frazzled and my relationship with the principal offered no support. One morning at work when I went to the toilet, I burst into tears. It frightened me greatly as I was unable to stop. I cried for at least ten minutes, maybe more. When I finally did stop, I went home for the day. The tears were involuntary like a dam that had burst. I saw a doctor, who insisted that I take a week off.

On the day of my return, I heard that a parent had accused me of doing something I would never do. I heard that Rad was furious and had not backed me up. I felt intense anger that after nearly two years he still doubted my integrity, so I threw my satchel the length of the corridor. When I retrieved my bag, I left my workplace and career behind.

In town, I ordered a beer; and it was the last drink I had for nearly eighteen years. No stress meant no need to intoxicate myself. The doctor insisted that I take the rest of the year off.

02 - Breakdown / Breakthrough

'When you give up everything, everything is yours.'
(Rumi)

Leaving the house I shared with Angie, I moved to the next town. *Wonthaggi* was an aboriginal name meaning 'home'. A friend from work let me live in his garden shed and I made the place cosy. After a few good sleeps I drew and painted as therapy and listened to soothing music. Alan lent me Astral Weeks, a record of the great Van Morrison. Hearing this music took me to me into a place that felt like actual heaven. In shock from recent events, Alan's kindness and Van Morrison's music became major supports for me.

I was exhausted on all levels. My body, my mind, my emotions, and my spirit were crushed. I had come to the point where reason had almost no value for me. I had given my utmost to teaching, but now I needed the company of angels and to celebrate my release.

I experienced a freedom that I had never known before, living barefoot in the garden, sleeping whenever I felt like it, and going for long walks into the local town. Sometimes complete strangers would come and take me to the beach for the day. I was living in my own version of Shangri-la.

I had walked away from my career and couldn't have been happier. For the first time in my life, I felt free of all the rules; inner as well as outer. I was in a world where everything went slowly and life itself was given full respect. I did, however, also feel like I had been hit by a train. I also felt as if there were bare loose wires in my brain, which sometimes shorted out. It is quite likely that, stopping work when I did, I had narrowly avoided permanent damage.

Alan's garden claimed me. I was intoxicated by its peace. The sunshine, the long grass, the health within the soil enchanted me. It was time for me learn about being close to nature. As I read about gardening, I planted seeds and tended to new growth.

I knew that I had lost contact with normality when my father phoned me and I wasn't able to have a conversation with him. The best I could do was hope that he knew how I felt. I put the phone to the stereo and left him listening to Jimmy Cliff singing, 'Where's the key that should unlock the door? ... sitting here by myself on the floor, with my head down in my hand.' I never asked him how he felt about that day, but both my parents came to visit me soon after that.

My parents looked quite concerned at the state of my health, while I did my best to convince them that I felt fantastic. My skin was almost translucent blue-white at the time, so I could understand why they were concerned. My health had gone but at the same time I had realised freedom. This sense of being released from the ties of old beliefs and social mores more than compensated for losing my health.

My ability to plan was also impaired. One afternoon, I had an inspiration to set up a business. At the local nursery I spent all the money I had left, purchasing ferns at retail price. I figured that I had an abundance of time so I could spend it propagating these beautiful plants. It wasn't until I got them home and began to read a book about them that I realised just how slowly they grew. It would take decades to grow more ferns and establish a business. I now had no money, but did have many beautiful plants to comfort me.

My brain was now quite disengaged from the world and worldly realities. Nothing bothered me except a deep anxiety that was beginning to invade my life from within. I had let go of many of my worries but I still had to deal with the consequences of my choices. I learned what it was to rest and felt what it was to be alive and live in complete surrender. I knew how rich this life is when we enter the Cosmic Dream. I had finally found something of my true nature and inner home. In that place I could exist as myself and not try to be anything for anyone else. It was a huge gift of Grace, yet I paid a high price for it.

Springtime brought many delights with the brilliant sunshine. My days in Alan's garden were glorious and many people who visited shared their treasures with me. Before long I knew how to grow vegetables, and was learning to listen to my intuition as well. I took to sitting naked on beaches, going for long swims, visiting the town, and enjoying the radiance of the sun. My health had well and truly gone but I was happy.

In the busyness of life I had lost contact with my peace. To get my health and balance back, I would need to live as simply as I could. It became obvious to me how much I had lost contact with the world when I got to the checkout counter at the supermarket one day. I had collected the things that I wanted but only then remembered that I needed to have money to pay for them. My mind had jettisoned some of the basic concepts of living in this world.

Daily waves of ecstasy came together with extreme lows. The highest highs and the lowest lows came and went without any warning. I often felt intense fear that developed into an ongoing anxiety of these attacks of mood. The worst was a fear of the fear, which started to wear me down. My emotions were virtually uncontrollable. It became a major focus for me just keeping myself afloat.

In realising my physical mortality, I became aware that I was infinite in spirit. It was an unusual business to awaken when so many others around me seemed to be asleep. I lived in a kind of sacred dreamtime, whereas others seemed to be lost in being practical. I was in my own paradigm, quite distant from the one most people inhabited. I could appreciate where I was, what I had, and the benefits of being left alone. But I know that I would not have survived without the kindness of my friends.

That Which Abides

Someone showed me how to read the *I-Ching* (Book of Changes) by using coins to create hexagrams with a corresponding text. My very first throw was *The Creative* – the first sentence in the book. It read: 'The clouds pass and the rain does its work, and all individual beings flow into their forms.' The text felt like acknowledgement from the Universe that I was being blessed with an entirely new beginning to life.

I increased my reading of Eastern thought, including Zen and the Tao. One sentence gave me great support and became the foundation of my focus for many years to come. It read: 'cling to that which abides.' The ups and downs of life would always be challenging and I could take refuge in something that was constant. I was now well aware that what truly abides is Spirit. In the following years I would also become aware of the truth of the adage: 'From fortune to misfortune is a very small step, but from misfortune back to fortune, can be a very long way.'
In Zen, I came across the writings of Suzuki Roshi. Roshi suggested that we find Nirvana when we realise that change is

one of the constants in life, and we find our bliss when we have composure in that knowing. This would be my practice.

In earlier days, I loved body-surfing in ocean waves. Back then I would take some calculated risks, swimming out to where waves were the biggest, and enter the exhilaration of riding them back to shore. Sometimes I would submit myself to the water nearer to the shore, allowing the waves to seize and drag me under into a thrashing whirlpool of white water. Now my health wouldn't allow it, so I enjoyed sitting on the shore instead. I found peace in watching others being active, and just observing the ways of life. I had to content myself with just being part of it without directly participating.

In simply being, I was more able to appreciate the beauty around me. Indeed, the old town where I now lived was very much like heaven on earth. Wonthaggi, for me, became like living a perfect dream: a country town where people went about their lives without stress. There was a relaxed building code and many houses still had rusty sheets of corrugated iron adorning them. The history and variety of Wonthaggi was presented to me like an art gallery of Australian beauty. The people of the town were pleasant to me and I felt accepted. I was fortunate to have found an environment where I could be and live in peace and stillness. My entire body came out in a skin rash, and I took this to be a manifestation of repressed emotions, making their way free.

Rock Pool

One day when I was on my own, I drove to the ocean, which was about half an hour from the town. The beach extended for many kilometres, yet I had it all to myself. I walked barefooted on the sand and came across a rock pool near the water's edge. Looking down I noticed a small crab going about its business. I was intent on watching what it was doing, when that tiny crab, some two metres from my eyes, suddenly looked up. It could not possibly have seen me, but it was aware of my attention on it. In the next moment, I became aware that above me, also beyond my physical vision, another consciousness was aware of me. I was in the middle of at least three worlds and was certainly not alone. This was the beginning of some quite unusual experiences. Most of them were pleasant.

I went to the edge of the water, watching the waves arrive and retreat. I noticed the point where the water generally stopped and returned. Something inspired me to place my forehead at that point. I stood on my head in a yoga headstand, and from there I observed the world upside down. The water sky came towards me. I watched and waited to feel what would happen next. To my great delight, when the edge of the wave reached me, it was with the most gentle of touches. It felt like I had just been baptised. The ocean touched my forehead and then returned from whence it came. That day gave me so many blessings, and, given my unusual state of mind, it was fortunate that I hadn't drowned.

The days were warm, and the opportunity to live quietly was healing. I'd heard about a man who was selling old train carriages and my dear friend Alan was happy for me to put one on his land. I cleared the back of his block, had a guard's van brought in, and then planted a cornfield around my new home.

Many people, who also enjoyed the simple lifestyle, began to visit me there. I loved their company and they were so kind. I had no idea where they came from but word of some kind must have gotten out. My life became quite social. My train carriage home often became open house in the afternoons to people from many walks of life: artists, a doctor, a botanist, an ex-prisoner, and other general wanderers and their friends. I had never met these people before and new company made for pleasant summery days. These were very special days for me.

An American botanist started visiting regularly. He would take me around town with him, as he researched what plants grew wild in the area. He taught me about me how plants behaved and offered me a very relaxing way of looking at the world. We sat in the full sun on the roof of my train carriage and he shared the ways in which he found the universe enthralling.

One day a doctor visited and took me to the beach with some of her friends. On the way she played a cassette tape of the music from the movie *Xanadu*. It wasn't my kind of music but I imagine she wanted to instill in me the message of the lyrics. To believe 'we are magic,' and that 'nothing can stand in our way.' It was an incredibly kind and loving gesture.

One man I met became a close friend. Sandy was a shark fisherman who also needed some time away from his job. He had recently had a narrow escape from being eaten by a huge shark and, like me, was in the process of healing his strained nerves. He showed me how to catch abalone, and then prepare and cook them on the beach. Sandy taught me to face my fears, spending whole days in the ocean. I snorkelled in the bull kelp, and sometimes followed him out into the deeper waters.

One day when we were in the ocean, half a kilometer off shore, I began to worry. We had simple spear-guns and it occurred to me that if one of us shot a fish, then surely its blood would attract a shark. When my heartbeat became louder than even my questioning thoughts, I decided to head back for shore.

Another day, Sandy called to me with great excitement. He was already in the water and encouraged me to jump in from the rocks. I dove into the water of a cove about four metres deep. Once I got in the water I realised what he was excited about. There were stingrays swimming around us. I had to assume that there was no real danger, as Sandy had called me in to experience this. It was pure wonder. Another day I swam above a stingray as it moved gently along the ocean floor. It was less than a metre beneath me and it is only now that I realize how dangerous that was.

I was enjoying spending my days in the ocean and becoming quite at one with all that I encountered. Most days I would spend six to eight hours in the water, and then throughout the night I continued to feel the ocean moving through me. I was regaining a sense of my body, a closeness with nature and freedom in life. Every day brought many new adventures.

Late one afternoon I was surprised by a visit from a friend of Sandy's, who had seen me at the local hotel. Elle just appeared at my door and declared that because we lived in the same part of town, I somehow belonged to her. It reminded me of the aboriginal concept of belonging to the land. Perhaps I belonged to Elle in the sense that I was part of her tribe. I appreciated her candour and we became close friends. Elle was a strong woman, but her whole life had recently been turned upside down.

Being with Elle released some past programs and helped me get closer still to my original nature. That night we made love on the beach, where the land met the crashing waves, and the starlight blessed us beneath the open sky. Elle was the earth to my air and helped me find balance and ease. I loved being with my new friends. They were from a whole different culture to what I had known before. In the afternoons we collected wild blackberries to make pies, and just enjoyed hanging out together.

One night, I went to the ocean with Elle and Sandy. At the beach, a mood overtook me and I felt that it was my time to leave this world. Despite my new life, my new friends and so many interesting adventures, something within me just wanted to die. I was often fighting uncontrollable fears and depression and these feelings drew me towards the black waves, while the others were playing around nearby. Sandy was doing cartwheels. Something in him must have sensed what was going on in me, and he cartwheeled across my path. His intervention stopped me and broke my attention from my heavy course. It was grace that he was there that night.

Sitting on the beach, surprised by what had happened, I saw a vision of my parents' faces, looking at me as if I had managed to die. I could see that they would not understand if I left like that. Their potential grief became my motivation to stay. For many years to come I would have to use such reasons to stay alive.

Elle had recently broken up with her partner, and was soon to leave the mainland. Everything in my life was ethereal and I thought I might enjoy going with her. It was to be an adventure that I was not at all prepared for.

I closed the doors of my train carriage, told Allan that I would return some day, and went off with Elle, her child, and one of her Elle's girlfriends We stayed in various people's houses in the city that week, and then boarded the overnight ferry to Tasmania. This was all quite disorienting for me. I was still recovering from losing my partner and my career, and now I had left my sanctuary as well. I took refuge in Elle's love, even though we had only known each for a couple of weeks.

I had very little money and no idea what I was getting myself into. I was happy to be in Elle's company and to be going on an adventure. In Tasmania we either pitched a tent, or just slept in any public buildings that could be used at the end of the business day. Elle had a cassette tape of Neil Young's album *Comes A Time* and this became our theme music. We sang throughout the day as we explored the Tasmanian back roads.

There was such a lovely feeling in the music and the company I kept. I got on well with Elle's young son and the four of us sang our hearts out. We were all fugitives in a way, temporarily escaping the collapse of our individual worlds. I could also feel that we were drifting and, at some point, I would need to settle again. My nervous system was shot and I began to feel the need for a steady home. I was enjoying myself but I was fragile and increasingly tested by fears.

At peace in the forest, sitting in the sun, a grasshopper sought my attention. It sat on my lower leg looking up, directly into my eyes. A clear connection was made. It was an unusual meeting between two different forms of creation. The grasshopper was so small, with its tiny eyes, but its consciousness wished to engage with mine. At that moment the grasshopper was more conscious than I was. Apart from my brief encounter with the crab, I had never before had such an intimate moment with a creature so small. I had always appreciated skinks, which seemed like symbols of the dreamtime, and the discovery of new varieties of insects, but had never felt they were intent on making direct contact with me. The time I had with this tiny creature opened my eyes. I was being called to be present with a wider world. The light of consciousness, within the grasshopper, was opening me to the oneness of all. It made me aware that this being and I were part of one thing. There was one Light in each of us and one consciousness in all things. In staying present with its invitation, I was awakened to a larger aspect of my whole self. Life was opening me up to it, and I saw no reason to not go with that. It was an unusual event but a very real one.

Squatting

We arrived in the township of Hobart and met some buskers in the city square. These fellow wanderers invited us to stay the night at their place. It was exciting to be part of a large household in which everyone came together in the evening to share whatever they had collected during the day. Various people arrived with diverse offerings: a block of cheese; some fruit juice; vegetables and eggs. All the food was put together into a communal meal, while the musicians entertained us and we shared our stories. There was extraordinary camaraderie amongst these gypsy people.

That night Elle and I had a whole bed to ourselves. It was my first night on a proper mattress in a long time. All night I felt like I was sleeping in midair. It was such a lovely experience. Living so simply gave many wonderful gifts.

The morning was another story. I was awoken by loud voices and the hectic movement of a dozen people throughout the house. When I got out of bed I was met by two large and imposing men. Someone relayed that the house belonged to the local university and that the authorities weren't impressed that we had been squatting. I was trying to remember what I had read about squatter's rights but these serious looking men were not about to discuss it. We moved quickly and got out into the new day, somewhat shaken but also quite amused.

Later in the day we met up again with the buskers, and they shared information about another house. It was about a half hour drive southeast of the city. The owner was a saxophone player, who had given his permission for it to be used while he was overseas. We gathered supplies and headed off to our new abode.

The house was solid and situated on the top of a hill, with a stunning view across the Snug Tiers. There was no furniture except a few blankets and mattresses but we happily settled in. There were the four of us who arrived from the mainland, as well as several other local travellers staying there. Previous visitors had developed a vegetable garden, and we helped look after this while we were there. It seemed that the house had become a shared project.

This collective style of living appealed to me. It was one of the points on my list of things that I wanted to learn about. People shared resources, skills, and varied interests. They also shared their joy and goodwill. We found all we needed at the local rubbish tip, including some very comfortable old car seats. These sat perfectly around our open fire, which was the place to be in the cool evenings.

Some enjoyed preparing food, others cleaning, and several of us liked building things. It was such a joy when everyone was doing whatever they felt like doing. There were no pressures of any kind. At various times other people would arrive and stay for a few days. I was learning to enjoy and appreciate being part of a large extended family.

Elle's child was around four or five years old. We often spent the days together and I did my best to be sensitive to what he was interested in. One day we found a dead chicken and buried it together. It felt supportive to show him that death was a natural part of life. One lesson included teaching him that when he defecated in his pants they had to be washed; so we washed them together. There wasn't a lot to do other than do whatever was needed in the moment. We often played games where we sang together and he loved to bash saucepans as part of the band. He was a natural drummer, but very challenging to my nervous system at the time. He naturally woke up every day at 5.00 am when I really need to sleep until after 9 o'clock.

We were deep in the Aussie bush and I surrendered to the simplicity of it all. In my spare time I found a great ally in reading Zen. Some of the poetry represented perfectly how I felt:

> *'The long night,*
> *the sound of water,*
> *says what I think.'*
>
> (Gochiku)

> *'Meeting, they laugh and laugh –*
> *The forest grove, the many fallen leaves.'*
>
> (From Zenrin Kushu)

And what I became, living in the forest hills:

> *'He thinks like the waves rolling on the ocean; he thinks*
> *like the stars illuminating the nightly heavens; he thinks like*
> *the green foliage shooting forth in the relaxing spring breeze.*
> *Indeed, he is the showers, the ocean, the stars, the foliage.'*
>
> (D.T. Suzuki)

My daily ritual included taking a wash in the rainwater drum, collecting firewood and doing maintenance or making things. When it rained I delighted in just standing under the hole in the roof gutter, letting the water pour down onto me from the open sky. When the moon was out I could wander in the forest at night amidst thousands of acres of natural blue gum bush. This was a time for learning to be at peace with myself and the Earth. With everything familiar now gone, I was learning to be grateful for what I had left.

The day came when I had to return to the mainland for some legal business. I had started a court case with the government over mistreatment at work. The Teachers' Union had taken up my case and I had to attend some interviews in the city. At the time I didn't feel it appropriate to invite Elle and her son to come and stay with my family, and I didn't have the means to accommodate them by myself. I felt torn leaving Elle behind but I needed to attend to business.

It was a bit of a strain having to be in the city for the week, sitting around in waiting rooms outside courtrooms. Day after day I did nothing, while solicitors spoke behind closed doors. I was pleased to get back to the wilds of Tasmania again.

When I returned I was informed that Elle had left for Papua New Guinea. It was difficult to comprehend this after we had been so close and shared such intimate times. Perhaps she was hurt by my actions, or just had a lot of inner pain and needed to keep on moving. Now I was living in a forest shack in the hills, in the south of Tasmania, without work, money, transport, or my usual friends.

I began to take prescription drugs for an increasing sense of anxiety. They were sleeping tablets, which were meant to help me relax. I relaxed so much that I nearly burned myself to death. Reading while in my sleeping bag, with a candle on my chest, I fell asleep and woke to see my chest on fire. I was so drugged that I could barely wake enough to put it out.

With no personal transport, I moved back into the township of Hobart, renting a room with some students there. I would occupy my days by walking along the bay, or through narrow alleyways in and out of the town.

One of my housemates studied at the local university. I contemplated enrolling in a course there and went in with him for the day. He was studying glass-blowing so I went to explore the visual arts facilities. I stood there in awe of the space and all the activity going on, until the head art teacher came over and stood before me. Without saying a word he adjusted his body shape to mirror mine. What he did shocked me, as I immediately became aware that my demeanour was like that of a cave man. I had let my appearance go. This teacher's simple action enlightened me to how the world perceived me. It was a jolt to my consciousness and another small awakening. I would need to make some changes.

I had been studying a book called *Survival into the 21st Century* and over time I was purifying my diet. I had been eating only fresh vegetables and fruit, and then only apples from the back yard garden. For some weeks I lived almost solely on alfalfa and mung bean sprouts, growing thinner by the week. On this diet my activities narrowed to meditation and some gentle yoga practices. I had very little energy for anything else.

At Easter on Good Friday I decided to climb Mount Wellington. I took my time walking very slowly. It took me the entire day and I thought about Jesus on the road to Calvary. It felt like there was very little left in my life except to work at regaining my health. After walking for the entire day and in pain most of the way, I stopped a few hundred metres from the peak. I had put myself through quite an ordeal but chose to deny myself the exhilaration of what would have been a breathtaking view. Exhausted and sore, I managed to hitchhike a ride back down to the town. Perhaps I wanted to experience something of the crucifixion. Quite possibly this was some baggage from misunderstanding the teachings put upon me in my youth.

I kept reading about Zen in all of its forms. Some of the poetry saved my life. The academic treatises were also very stimulating. Zen helped me to see beyond my exhausted body and fragile mind, and to find my peace in being still and aware.

Zen made me accept the lost connections, and I was able to relax in my current circumstances. It helped me be okay with my ruined health, and my loss of direction. It taught me how suffering is created and perpetuated by the mind. Zen helped me to begin to return to my essential, true nature. For me, at that time, Zen was all I needed to find peace, and to acknowledge that all my needs were always met. In any given moment, there was nothing lacking.

My new friend, Christian, had a car, and took a group of us to visit some of the most exquisite nature in the south of Tasmania. It was on one of these days that I received an inner message that I was in paradise but that, at some point soon, I would need to return to society. It was clear to me that knowing paradise wasn't right without sharing this knowledge with others. I had a duty to share my awareness with greater humanity.

My time in Tasmania was coming to a close. I heard of a healing festival that was to be held in Tannelorn in the warmer climes of New South Wales. I headed back to Victoria to visit my family and then hitchhiked the 1,100 kilometres north.

In those days my wardrobe consisted of one pair of shorts, a short-sleeved woollen grandfather-shirt, and one woollen jacket. The woollen Jacket was good for when it rained; wet or dry, it kept me warm. It also became my pillow each night. Midwinter,

I purchased a second grandfather shirt and wore as many layers as were required. I also had a small survival space-blanket that could double as a raincoat and warming device. I owned one pair of massage-sandals but I went most places barefoot.

I travelled very lightly and procured myself a small tent. Hitch-hiking, I met an array of my countrymen and women. The majority of rides involved being a good listener. People who gave me a lift often wanted to share their philosophies on life. Sometimes I got to share my own as well but more often I paid for the ride by just being a good listener for the driver. I had recently had my hair dyed bright green so some of the rides were from people who just wanted to give me their opinion about that.

The festival was held on a farming property not too far from the East Coast. The organisers had an interest in exploring alternative lifestyles. Tannelorn drew people from many walks of life, including healers and massage therapists, motor-bike riders, various religious groups, rain-dancers, new agers and the Australian music industry. For five days we were part of a social experiment to see how people could live together in harmony, in the hope that we would inspire improvements in our general culture.

From the alternative music stage, one day, I heard a choir singing. I was relaxing in the river when I heard angelic voices floating through the air. The sound of this choir radiated a keynote of pure love, which took me by surprise and was completely intoxicating. I ran to get closer to the singers. At that moment I knew there was something much higher than I had ever experienced before. I knew that it was possible for me to find a spiritual bliss.

Tannelorn offered workshops and I attended many of them. One included how to live on wild foods in the Australian bush. The man offering this workshop lived on a commune called the Garden of Eden. He was sitting on a rock in the river when I met him. He radiated a deep peace and his eyes shone brightly. When I looked into his eyes I couldn't find his pupils. His eyes were like a night sky with thousands of stars. I didn't understand it except to acknowledge that he was an exceptional being and that this was a special meeting. It was as if he didn't really belong to this world and had somehow gone beyond it. There was no idle chatter in his mind or between us. I sensed that I had met someone who was in unity with all of nature.

At that time, I was being awakened to various realms of consciousness that I had not been aware of before. I was slowly losing contact with mainstream society, and meeting something of what was out there in the wider domain. This man, with the starry eyes, and many others had found what I had been looking for: an incredibly deep peace that came from a wellspring within.

That night I attended another workshop, which was also to do with living close to the land. I learned a technique for surviving if naked in the wild. By covering one's body in mud, which hardens, a barrier to the wind is created. The mud forms a coat that keeps the body's warmth in. In my coat of dried mud I wandered with the workshop facilitator, visiting many of the other events that night. Being a naked mud-man was yet another a new experience for me.

In the sunshine the next day, I passed a woman who smiled at me. Her eyes lit up with love and I felt, for a moment, a sense of living in an elevated state. She radiated so much love that it had me wondering if I could even cope in a perfect world.

I wondered how humanity would behave, if everything were blissful all the time. I was taken aback by the love this woman had bestowed on me.

At the conclusion of the five days most people headed back to wherever they had come from. I stayed on an extra day and relaxed in the river. I noticed that as the people left, the animal life returned. While floating on my back, a snake swam past near my face. The snake had no concern about me. It seemed to be at ease because I was as well.

While relaxing in the river I floated and played like a seal. I moved my arms so that my body would turn along its central axis. While I did this, I noticed a series of lights within my body. I began to have visions of geometrical forms and structures made of light. These continued for a short while, changing shape as I continued to move. I have been privileged on many occasions, to be shown such fascinating phenomena.

Returning Home

After Tannelorn, I headed back to Victoria. By now I was used to hitchhiking and taking every day as it came. I enjoyed meeting new people as well as keeping to myself. My personal anthem was Freeborn Man by Ewan MacColl. I had known this song for many years but now it resonated fully with my wandering lifestyle. Ewan celebrated: 'There was open ground where a man could linger.

Stay a week or two for time was not your master. ...' In those days it was easy to wander. Australia was still quite undeveloped with great open lands. You could sleep under a bush, pitch your tent by a river, and go wherever you pleased. It was a special time being able to walk the paths that the ancestors had walked before, in a land where a man or woman was free to go walkabout like a sage or sadhu.

I often thought that we would be okay as a nation, if we just made sure that walkabout was kept as a right for all. Also, I believed that our beaches and rivers should remain free. Protecting them from individuals and corporations who might seek ownership. I continue to hope that this may be so.

In one year I had forty-one different abodes and began to feel that it was time to settle down. Back in Victoria, I visited my old friends. Alan was happy for me to stay with him again. I visited familiar places and, to my surprise, people I had been close to didn't recognise me. In the past year I hadn't cut my hair or shaved so I looked nothing like the person they had known. I had anonymity in my own town, and it felt very safe. The anonymity gave me a free space where I could wander without being challenged about my past. I was free to be.

Some of my dearest friends were the people I had taught with. One of them was in charge of a local program for educating unemployed youth at an institution I had worked at before. To my delight he offered me a paid job there. Another friend who worked at the school convinced me to go back there with her one evening. In walking the halls I could feel that I had regained something of my strength again. I could face my past and let it go. It was healing to reconnect with the place again, but without the stress that had broken me a year before.

On leaving the building, I noticed Rad in his office working late. He invited me in for a chat and we got on well. It was a pleasant surprise to be able to relax with him. On sharing with him that I had been offered a job he suddenly became furious. The funding for the program went through the school accounts and he told me he would block the supply if I accepted the job.

The job would have helped me re-engage with work and settle again in my hometown but that opportunity was gone in seconds. I knew that I could not accept the work now, as it would mean being at war with Rad again. I left that night in shock. My bridges burned, I knew that I had to move again.

My plan had been to rebuild my health and to get back to work, but the meeting with Rad had thrown me. We had never understood each other's motives but it was hard to believe he was now directly interfering in my life. I decided to continue with the legal action. The Union offered to back me, and I eventually won the case after five years.

Perhaps Rad and I had past life wounds, which might now carry over to yet another life. Ideally, I like to think that we were two old warriors with much to learn who gave each other some good life lessons.

One of the main lessons I learnt from that time was to seek harmony. This would put me in good stead for future opportunities.

03 - Making Connections

Shocked and wounded, I contemplated seeking shelter in a mental hospital. I wrote a letter to a local psychologist, proposing that I be employed because of my unique situation and education, but did not receive a reply. My second option was to attend art school. I applied to the visual arts institute where Angie had studied. Accepted into the course, I decided to focus on ceramics. This would give me contact with the elements of earth, water, air and fire, as well as my creative spirit. I hoped that the practice of making pots would be a meditation as well as a discipline.

For a while it was easy and fun. I got to work with clay on a daily basis, and I reconnected with my body and hands. I loved working in the ceramics studio and with the other people I met there. Many of them were very chilled. They had their personal projects, and quietly worked towards creating what they had in their hearts and minds. One evening outside of class time, the technician taught me how to make a pinch pot. This involved making coils of clay and then joining them one on top of the other, circle upon circle, until they made the shape you wanted. I built one as tall and wide as myself, and then made a bonfire in it. The experience connected me with my love of traditional African culture and dance. We also worked with a Japanese technique called *Raku*. We fashioned pots from clay that could withstand high thermal shock. These could be fired immediately and intensely and then thrown into a bucket of water with an explosive effect. Appropriately, the word Raku is Japanese for 'enjoyment.'

Another great pleasure in ceramics was the fellowship of artists. When a group was firing its work in a kiln, we would often sit together throughout the night. It was such a grand occasion to sit around the warmth of the fire, waiting for our creations to be born. Much care had gone into the making of the pots but in the firing of them the final result was up to nature.

Creating art and working with my hands was very satisfying and I could feel it helping me to heal. I also enjoyed the indoor heated swimming pool nearby. At the beginning of each day at around 7:00 a.m., I would walk ten minutes down the country road and have the whole pool to myself. I didn't have the energy for swimming laps, so my favourite activity was to play at being a whale or a dolphin and to move the way they might move, waving my flippers and enjoying deep dives. Letting all the air out of my lungs I could sink to the bottom of the pool. I made noises and listened to the effects. I dove deep, enjoying feeling the weight of my body as it sank. I could wait on the bottom of the pool until it became essential to return for air. The attendants got used to me so I didn't have to worry that they might think I was drowning. Every morning, for that hour or so, I played in bliss.

Despite the fun, my anxiety was still present and increasing. I began to take the prescription drugs again, which pushed me into an uncomfortable altered state. When I took the prescribed amount I felt only mild help but increasing the dose simply increased disconnection from my feelings. I became like a zombie, living in a body with a mind that floated somewhere behind my eyes. I felt trapped deeper inside myself and even less able to negotiate with the world. I guess it helped that I was at an art school where it didn't seem to matter as much.

I was having trouble finding regular accommodation until I managed to organise a dormitory room connected with the institute. It worked well for a while but then I began feeling uncomfortable there. I had become one of the main cooks of the evening meals but the drugs made me feel less able to socialise. I began trying to avoid others in the common room, entering and leaving via my bedroom window. The way I withdrew into my private cave reminded me of a movie called *Themroc*. The administration became aware of my behaviour and one night I came home to find that they had secured bars across the window. Now I could only access my room if I went through the front door, which became too difficult for me.

Giving up my room, I took to sleeping on the concrete floor under the seat at the local bus shelter. I knew that I wouldn't be able to do it for long. I soon found a hammock in the small rotunda in a common space between the classrooms. The hammock was comfortable enough with a roof overhead but there were no walls. It was protected from most rain and dew but the air coming through was very cold. Each night, around two or three in the morning, the security officer made his rounds and I had to move. This further compromised my health, as I was never able to get a full night's sleep.

I enjoyed the contact with the night sky but was becoming more and more feral. After a while I realised that I could sleep underneath an office desk inside the main building but I still had to move around in the middle of the night to avoid being caught. I also gained access to one of the other buildings, where I found a space to sleep on the concrete floor under the studio sink. My accommodation became more and more basic, and less advantageous to my health. After several months of shifting around campus, I felt worn out and decided to move on completely. I would have loved to continue my studies there but I simply couldn't manage. I felt homeless and unable to find my sanctuary.

I was tired and frail but my hopes were aroused again when I heard of another alternative festival to be held within the state. This was a *ConFest*, a conference-festival, to be held near the town of Glenlyon. I pitched my tent and woke to meet 4°C. It was cold and dark and I couldn't sleep. I went for a wander through the campsite, and noticed ten or so people sitting on the ground in a circle. They were very friendly and indicated that I was welcome to join them. It was still around half an hour before the sun would rise and they were singing mantric songs of devotion and invocation. The words 'Baba Nam Kevalum' were repeated over and over and created the deepest sense of peace within me. The words meant something like: 'Love is the essence of all things.' A violinist in the group played in a way that drew me inwards and upwards. There was something about his playing that connected me directly with spirit. The sounds seemed to dance with the angels, and lifted me to a higher plane. I was in a divine place.

Most of the people present were dressed in orange clothes and were part of a spiritual group. It was interesting how mentally clear they were, unlike most of the people I had met. The experience was so uplifting that I begged the yogi to teach me how to play the violin the way he did. The teacher acknowledged my interest and said that first I would have to give away all that I owned and be completely free of all attachments to the material world. Once I had done that, I was welcome to approach him again and to concentrate all my efforts into yogic meditation and violin.

I so dearly wanted to accept his offer but could feel that it was not my right path at that time. However, it made me more aware of my true path and gave me a lot to think about. That morning had further awakened me to what was possible on a spiritual path but I knew that I had to approach it from another direction. I could feel that my spiritual practices lay elsewhere.

A Fight for Health

I headed for the ocean to build my strength. For motivation, I read a book on the SAS (Special Air Services) and began to train myself like a soldier might. I pushed myself to my physical limits and did everything I could to improve my diet. I had stopped taking the prescription drugs and began an apple juice fast for purification. What should have been a three day cleanse I continued for many months. By the time I realised what I had done, I was as skinny as Mahatma Gandhi. I finally acknowledged that I needed help and sought further medical advice.

A local chiropractor, well known for helping people with health issues, encouraged me to imagine what I could create. He worked on my spine and put me on a diet rich in nutrients. He renewed my hope and blessed me on my way.

Feeling stronger, I left the beach to live in the wooded hills of Mt. Dandenong, an area half an hour west of the city and covered in native forest and introduced species. Many houses had at least an acre of land around them and the rest was mostly state forest. It was a haven away from a busy world.

I managed to stay there for some years, tending to an acreage garden and building up my various strengths. The air was purified by the forest and quite invigorating. I lived on a simple diet and continued my studies in Zen. I also investigated macrobiotics, living mainly on brown rice, seaweed and pickled radish. A naturopath warned me that if I didn't change this diet, I would end up only being able to relate to Japanese monks! The longer I kept to myself the more obscure my life became.

For three years I didn't speak to anyone. Apart from an occasional visit from my parents, I kept completely to myself. I even avoided contact with the cashiers at the supermarkets when I purchased my food. In the end I felt so isolated that I needed to park my van in the shopping centre car park, just to feel that I was with people. I had access to radio and often listened to talkback at midnight, hearing a minister speaking with people who reached out for help via the program. His caring and advice to these people also felt supportive for me.

I took to wandering barefoot in the forests, usually in the evenings as it became dark. Often it would rain and I found it fascinating to commune so closely with the forest world. I could study the beauty of nature's form in ferns, large trees and wild mushrooms. For some time I was intrigued with being alone and sensing the very nature of nature.

The place became even more special during the winter when the ground was covered in snow. As the light faded, the white snow contrasted brilliantly with the black outline of trees. When I drove at night I drove slowly, listening to Dire Straits singing 'Brothers In Arms'. This accentuated the beauty and mystery of the experience. Marc Knopfler's guitar took me deeper within myself. At home in the cottage, I explored making sounds on a simple Quena flute. My only two LP records were of whales singing in the ocean. I was living in a floating world.

I had well and truly cut my connections with society and was regressing ever deeper. My closest and most cherished companions became the flowers in the garden. Once a year, for less than a week, the cherry blossom tree would burst forth its blooms. When the wind struck the tree, my entire field of view became pink blossoms. These occasions would inspire a mild ecstatic state within me.

I came to see that I had previously placed too much trust in humanity and then had lost it all in one go. At some stage I would need to trust again, especially to find some balance. I had been too idealistic in my youth, and had since given up on my quest to awaken the world to greater love. The idea that finally got me moving was something I read about one day: atrophy. I hadn't touched anyone in years and this realisation shocked to me into seeking company again.

I sought more professional help and it was my great fortune to meet a wise psychologist. What first impressed me about him was that he had a lock on the door of his office to which only he had a key. I was confronted with the idea that I could also have such clear personal boundaries. I didn't have to withdraw entirely to be allowed to make such choices about my personal space.

I met with this man for only one hour and he helped me begin a whole new path in life. At the end of the session he spoke to me of Carl Gustav Jung. The psychologist recommended that I read Jung's book titled *Memories, Dreams and Reflections*. He also told me to go home and observe my dreams.

I relished the book and, not being one to ever do things by halves, spent the next six months mostly sleeping so I could

57

do as he recommended. It was mid winter and conducive to staying in bed and hibernating. I learned a lot about the nature of dreams at that time. I also explored the use of various herbs recommended in my botanical medicine studies, to assist in my research. What mysteries of the human condition could I access through investigations in the dream state? This question became a major enquiry at the time.

In reading Jung I found a soulmate, especially in his sharing about dispelling negative beliefs that were held about God. This brilliant book helped me to let go of old paradigms that I had been cajoled into accepting in my early schooling. Jung's writings worked as a welcome and powerful catalyst to release some of the old beliefs I still held.

By following my dreams, I began to see how varied and helpful they could be. In sleeping for that half year, I saw many symbols and structures within my psyche. I saw inner events, and I was able to move beyond beliefs that had held me back for many years. Freeing myself from some old ways helped me get closer to who I really was. I was also supported by the writings of Theosophist Annie Besant, especially that: 'There is an end to sorrow. With the ceasing of ignorance shall come the end of pain.'

I continued reading about Zen, Tao and I-Ching, while spending my days in the forests. I read Sufi poetry, Dervish stories and other esoteric texts. Some days I would work in the garden, raking leaves and pruning overgrown trees. Each day I would dedicate some quiet time to clearing the stone paths. When the sun was out, I would lie naked in the open air to receive its rays. Whenever there were storms, I would delight in walking amidst the powerful natural forces. I wanted to feel at one with nature and indeed it was my whole world for a time.

One morning, at the end of a dream, I saw a vision of myself in a prison cell. When I looked away from the bars at the window, I could see that I was free to walk out. The door was open. Unconsciously, I had imprisoned myself for years, probably out of guilt for having failed at being a teacher. In a cell of my own making, I had played judge, jury and jailer. I had set myself a limited life, and had been bound by it for many years.

For whatever reason, I had given up on life. The suicidal tendency that was there when I first left my work was still present to a degree. I had regressed so far into myself that one night a cloud of darkness formed overhead in the sky. This energy called to me that my time had come. It was enticing me to my death but I refused its unwelcome presence and continued to established myself more and more in being conscious and alive

Seeking Sanctuary

It was around this time that I began to visit and stay briefly with my parents. The voices in my head were still a constant, and they would tell me what to do and where to go. For instance, after hours of preparations to go to the suburbs, on the way there the voices would tell me to return to my country retreat. The voices were not my ally and eventually I took a stand that I would not follow any of their guidance, unless it came in the form of full body knowing. I would not act unless I could feel within my whole being that something was true. I was learning to ignore the war in my mind and to attune to my intuition instead.

At my parents' house I would sit in their garden and just go within. It had been many years since I felt like I had a home, and during that time I sought to find my place of peace. In meditating I would regularly pray to be able to find my sanctuary. On several occasions I partially blacked out, becoming dizzy and falling over, still cross-legged but lying on my side on the deck. At these times I was connecting to some higher energy force within me, and I intuited that the sanctuary I sought was within me. The sanctuary I yearned for was already mine. It was waiting for me to access higher aspects of my own being.

A very dear friend from school days came to visit me but I was unable to speak. I now lived mostly inside my own world and, though I greatly appreciated seeing him, I could not bring myself to talk that day. It was sad not being able to communicate with such an old friend but I felt there was nothing to say. I was gravely concerned at how he would take me not speaking with him. Years later he confided that he had also, at one stage, experienced a similar state, when the brain stops working in its usual way and other realms are revealed.

I became concerned with how other people were experiencing me, so I developed a practice where I would explain myself whenever I could. If I was leaving the room, I would announce where I was going. I didn't wish to create any confusion in others who could not comprehend my general silence.

This text by Saint-John Perse expressed perfectly the state that I had been in for several years.

'Leave me now, I'm going alone.
I'm going because I've business: an insect waits to deal with me.
I feel a joy in that great faceted eye, sudden as cypress fruit.
Or else, I've a union with the blue-veined stones:

> *so, leave me just the same,*
> *sitting in the solace of my knees.'*

> (Saint-John Perse, Elogues XVIII. Translation)

Madness

One day while taking in the Sun, something significant occurred. I was sitting on the edge of my parents' balcony when I became aware, out of the blue, that I had gone mad. I had contemplated madness and lunacy for many years, thinking I would come to understand it and be able to help people. But now I was not merely investigating it; I was in it. I was mad.

I experienced the madness as though, without my knowledge, I had dropped below the surface of the ocean and was now too deep to be able to get back up. I knew that if I didn't surface soon, I would lose connection to life altogether, and that if this occurred I would not be able to re-establish consciousness again. I would be lost. It was the most frightening experience I ever had. In almost that same instant, it was as if I shot to the surface, bursting forth and gasping the precious air. One split second after I was aware of the danger of eternal madness, I was freed from it. It had frightened me to my core, and I chose to never go anywhere near there again. The experience was enough motivation to go forwards for the rest of my life.

I focused on getting myself stronger and every night I ran for hours through the hills. I made an exercise plan and spent many hours every day building my fitness. I walked or rode my bike, as well as running up and down stairs with weights on my back. In sitting quietly and observing my mind, I got to see how thoughts would just come and go. I noticed how easy it was to become attached to those thoughts and to assume they were real. In observing the mind, I was able to become free of it to a degree. The main practice for me was to just allow the thoughts their own life but not to attach anything to them. I could see how they were the stuff of illusion.

On the balcony by the cherry blossom tree, one day, I sat quietly following my breath. In an instant I lost awareness and went within. In this inner space, I was without consciousness. In my physical body I sat still and immoveable. In this practice 'I' became nothing at all. 'I' ceased to exist. Beyond ego, beyond thought, beyond any consciousness at all, I was safe. My life force went to a place beyond cognition. I don't know how long I was in this state but when I returned, I became aware of 'a' nose on the front of 'a' face. The face, I then realised, was 'mine.' I knew that 'I' had returned. From being in that other place, I came back to being conscious again. This process was similar to what happens in waking from sleep, but now I was conscious of the process.

I read, in a book on Zen, that this was a relatively common experience amongst practitioners. It was a very special moment and I experienced it in deep peace. It was as if I had learned to travel between dimensions.

This experience encouraged me to continue my explorations. I imagined how one day, when the practices were more integrated within me, I could return to the world at large. I was learning how to go beyond my ego self, and find strengths and clarity regardless of stress. I was learning how to respond to life in any given moment. I could choose my path and my attitudes, rather than just re-acting old programming. Perhaps I had found what I needed to withstand the insanities that I perceived in the world at large. I was finding sanctuary: within my own being, in nature and many of the Eastern philosophies, and in the way of the spiritual warrior. I had been on a search for a higher code that I could live by and I was gradually finding it.

By now, very little surprised me in life. After living alone for six years, I became focused on what I might need to do next. I wondered if I could get a seat in the government Senate, in order to push for laws to protect and establish more National Parks. I realised that to have any chance of this path in life, I would have to begin speaking with people again. I forced myself to get out during the day and talk to people about my ideas. I received some positive feedback and saw it as a possible course, but not a probable one. At least it was something that motivated me to be with people again.

My father had worked for much of his life and was soon to retire. On the day he retired, I felt an inner shift in my energy, insisting I return to worldly duties. It felt as if my father had placed a flag in the sand, and I had to pick it up and carry it now. I was called into service. Nothing was said between us, but I knew that my outer work had begun again.

The exceptional and extraordinary were now just part of my daily life.

Group Therapy

Her name was Amy and in a one-hour therapy session she heard everything that I had needed to say to someone for six or more years. With empathic listening, Amy helped me cross a major hurdle – and leave the Rubicon.

I joined her regular group therapy sessions, which helped me learn to be with other people again. It also helped train me to be sensitive to the needs of self and others. Therapy involved speaking openly and honestly in a group where participants and therapists gave me their full support. I could discuss any issue whatsoever and it helped me to clarify what had held me back for so many years.

Amy identified that I had been forcefully repressing my resentment towards Rad. Trying not to harm him had taken all of my inner resources. I had been in an inner battle to neutralize myself, which was part of what I had seen in my prison dream.

I continued to attend the therapy sessions and met many others who were also on difficult healing paths. It was reassuring to see that I was not alone. Also, in being part of a group, I was privileged to share other people's journeys, and be supportive of their eventual breakthroughs. So much was shared and so deeply. Just the way I liked it.

The time came for me to leave my retreat and to re-enter the world at large. I had explored all that I needed in this sacred 'time out'. I had learnt much from my dreams, found balance through my connection to nature, and I had seen how suppressed anger had been ruining my life.

Having gathered my things to leave the cottage, I looked across at the lounge room and saw a single word. It appeared in mid air, large across the room. It was a key for me for the next stage of my journey and all it said was 'Acceptance.' I had to accept all that had gone before and all that was now, or ever would be. In being willing to adopt the lesson of acceptance, I could truly be free. More than twenty years later, this is still a major lesson, and support in my life.

Lama Choedak, in relaying a message from H.H. 14, the Dalai Lama, said:

> *'... Laughter is actually learning how to move on, and*
> *not blame the river which drowned your shoes last year.*
> *When that river is not there. That river would have long gone,*
> *and merged with the main ocean.'*

My Own Home

In 1987 I moved to the Melbourne suburbs. I had my own apartment at the rear of a house, a space looking onto a garden, privacy from public life. The house was situated very close to the Bay and from the front gate it was only a five-minute walk to the water. On any day I could go to the beach and wander for hours, or sit on a rock at the water's edge. I had nothing to do but relax and continue to heal.

I loved the beach but some days found it almost impossible to get there. It was only after I moved into the house that symptoms of agoraphobia presented. I hadn't experienced this level of fear for nearly six years. On many days, I wasn't even able to walk past the end of the driveway.

I experienced overwhelming fears, some of which seemed to come from my childhood. If I was walking along the footpath and someone was coming the other way, I felt I needed to cross the road to avoid any contact. Otherwise, I would 'have to' engage and be nice to them, and I didn't feel comfortable with this. I felt intimidated by all the rules and manners I had taken on as a child. There was something about set ways of doing things that made me feel like my freedom was being taken away.

I decided that I could not let the phobia get the better of me or my life would no longer be my own. I committed to seeing through small tasks that I set for myself, such as going to the beach, even if it meant many avoidance strategies along the way. After some practice, with my near-to-home beach journeys, I felt confident enough to take this further. I enrolled in Tai Chi classes and made a commitment to attend for the next four weeks. For my practice, I had to attend these classes, no matter how severe the symptoms became. Once I achieved a small goal, I could recommit to an extension of this. I needed to rebuild trust in myself and know that I could make a decision and stick to it.

On the day of the first class I managed to force myself to go from my car into the building, and then part way down the hall. I took refuge in the toilet, and then pushed myself to go the rest of the way into the class itself. I had to go through most of this again for the second class and at the beginning of that class the fear rose up suddenly and I nearly blacked out. Following through with my commitment to facing these debilitating fears, they gradually loosened their grip and I became relatively free.

Tai Chi became a major support for me and I practiced it every day for the next three years. I could tell in the very first class that Tai Chi was something I could do for the rest of my life and still not realise all of its secrets. It was fascinating to me, and it gave stability and depth to my life.

The Augustine Centre

I still felt somewhat lost in life and attended a local career counsellor. His first impression of me was that I belonged in Kabuki theatre, on stage. This reminded me of how much I had loved being in the theatre and it momentarily restored my sense of being larger than life. Acting was definitely in my heart and in my blood at that time. At Teachers College, I had played many roles: the tragic king in Euripides' Bacchae, an improvised performance of Shakespeare's Hamlet, and many other roles. I had played two characters in prison plays, with performances in three major gaols, including a maximum security gaol. I had also performed several characters in a trilogy of the Polish absurdist movement and taken part in major dance performances. It had been such an intense and brilliant part of my life. This man's single comment reminded me of a time when I had been fully and passionately alive. The thought of theatre stirred my blood and I enrolled in a course called Playback Theatre.

The Augustine Centre for Drama and Growth was an old church that had been converted to a personal development centre. It still held services in a Sunday morning group and ran many classes in creative and healing processes. One of the most endearing aspects of Augustine was its community. Many participants volunteered their time, tending to the gardens or contributing to maintenance. The staff, facilitators and teachers were also of very kind hearts, and often seemed filled with playful joy.

The Playback Theatre was something more far-reaching than I had expected. It gave me the opportunity to feel joy again. The games and role-plays awakened me to the depths of creative fun. Each session included one participant offering an issue of importance from their life. Then the other participants would become characters in a scene and act out the issue. The person who had raised the issue would direct each actor, choosing their role and suggesting their lines. Then it was open for all involved, to play, interact, and see what insights each person gained in their role. In Playback I got a sense of interest and involvement in life again. I also 'fell in love' with the teacher.

I can see now how I was merely projecting the unexpressed love within me towards the person who was helping me the most. I lay my heart at her feet but her response was very blunt. She had no romantic interest in me whatsoever. I had not entertained the possibility of that kind of response and it came as a shock. I sat quietly with the rejection, until I realised what a gift she had given me with her clear and honest reply. Jenny helped me to come back to reality. Her honesty and strength helped me to awaken from my unfounded fantasies.

Thankfully this episode didn't interfere with my continued attendance at Playback. I loved the classes, and still felt my heart being re-awakened in Jenny's presence. I was clear about my projections on her, and made the most of the many gifts that the sessions bestowed.

I soon added classes in Creative Expression, Conflict Resolution, Drawing on the Right Side of the Brain, Movement Ritual and Soul Dance. I also attended several private classes including a Shiatsu diploma course. Once I got going I was attending classes five days a week, in addition to my Shiatsu classes all day Saturdays. On Sundays I joined in the Morning Group, which was run in association with the Uniting Church.

The Centre gave me somewhere to go, and the chance to develop my personal and social skills. I worked in the garden as well as painting most of the workshop rooms. Peter, the administrator, organised many tasks for me to do and shared some of his wonderful philosophies with me. On days when I began rushing about, Peter would calmly ask me: 'What have you lost?' I would continue rushing, replying, 'I haven't lost anything, I'm just looking for the tools.' On my next passing of his office, he would again gently question: 'What have you lost?' It took me awhile to realise that he was identifying that I had lost my quietude.

I relished three full years at Augustine as I rebuilt my new life. Movement classes with Tony became a major part of my healing journey. Two evenings a week I danced for several hours. Tony organised musicians to come and play live, which inspired how we danced. His love of expressive movement was greatly supportive for me.

In one of the sessions I experienced a major release of fear. Tony introduced an exercise that focused on opening and closing. During the session it was up to us when and how much we opened or closed ourselves. This was in direct contrast to some of the triggers of my agoraphobia at that time. In opening and closing as I chose, I felt an almost immediate reprogramming of my mind and a reconnecting to my life as being my own. Such a simple exercise activated healing in my body-mind, and opened me to whole new possibilities.

The classes also gave me back my love of painting. Often we did free drawing after we had danced. Then we used the images as stimuli for further inspiration to move. We were encouraged to draw freely using oil pastels. The free movement and subsequent dance, opened me up for my creativity to flow. Moving and drawing so freely felt like a release from some of the restrictions that had been overlaid early on during school programming. Rather than being told what to draw and how to make it look real, it was all real. The action was the art. I began drawing most days, expressing energies that had been trapped since early primary school. Sometimes I drew my anger; other days I explored more subtle feelings. Sometimes I just enjoyed what happened when I played with colours. The sessions brought me back to my senses, and my senses brought me back to life. Many days it was just like the freedom of kindergarten again. I could be 4 years old and true to myself.

It was also in these classes where I began having visions while I danced. It was not uncommon for me to see giant flowers and waterfalls, and possible past-life experiences. On one occasion I saw people being shot at by a fighter plane, and I was the pilot. This was a little bit too real for my liking at times. I also experienced various other cultures within me while I danced. Most of these paranormal experiences felt okay, but sometimes they could become overwhelming. When this occurred, I had to stop moving for a while and come back to my breath and physicality. For this, I immediately took the yoga position of *Mud asana* - curled up, head over knees, in a bowing position on the floor. Then I would lie there until the visions passed. I also began having visions in my day-to-day life as well.

This was an expansive time for me. I attended Postural Integration, deep-tissue massage sessions, as well as participating in a six month course in Tantra yoga. On the Tantra weekends we learned about meditation and other awakening exercises. The weekends were held in the country, and I loved the special space that was created at each session. I very much enjoyed being the first to wake in the mornings, and light the wood fire for the day. Contributing to the well-being of others by warming our workshop room felt like a sacred act to me.

The Tantra involved varied practices, including special breathing techniques, and active imagination exercises. In many of these, the visualisations stimulated strong visions in me. In one meditation while sitting with a straight back, I saw hundreds of small lights racing back and forth within my body. The facilitator commented on the profound peace I had been in at the time. I also had a shocking experience where I felt and saw myself as an African warrior at the moment of being killed. It was very graphic and confronting. The tantric practices opened me up to many previously unknown worlds.

Around this time I would go for walks along the beach where I lived. One evening I walked for around half an hour when I felt that I should stop. I practised Tai Chi for a while, enjoying finding my balance with the shifting sand beneath my bare feet. Before me was the afterglow of a beautiful sunset.

The sky was incredibly rich and full, in a mixture of colours, predominantly blues. The water was reflecting what was left of that day's light. What happened next was a surprise. There was a Presence coming through the entire scene. Everything before my eyes, except this Presence, was shown to be an illusion. Everything that I could see was now obviously a mere backdrop to reality. There was a voice that came with the Presence. There were no drugs involved and this was completely real to me. For a moment, I was given the grace of seeing something behind the veil of illusion.

I found myself opening to many different experiences at that time and wanted to continue this unusual education.

04 - The Mountain

The phone rang. It was Neri and she was her usual bright self. She was organising a trek in Nepal, and asking if I was interested in going. I had been contemplating this for years but the invitation came out of the blue. I felt I needed time to think about it but, after I hung up the phone, it was less than a minute before I called her back with an enthusiastic 'Yes!'

Something about Nepal had called to me for some time. It bothered me that for most of my life I had not managed to complete anything. This was part of my motivation. I felt the need to begin the climb and see it through to the end.

There were many preparations before we left, including increasing my training regime. I began by returning to Mt. Dandenong each week and walking 'the thousand steps' with weights in my backpack. I purchased waterproof boots and walked each day to wear them in. The journey would be difficult enough without any issues with my equipment.

One of my main fears about going on such a journey was that my ankle might give way in the mountain wilderness. My fears were realised the very weekend before we left, not high up in the Himalayas but at our send-off party. Incredibly, one of Neri's friends was a physiotherapist and she was able to work on my ankle at the party. Having already experienced something of my fear, I felt confident that it probably wasn't going to be an issue after all.

The day before I left, my friend Peter whispered in my ear: 'Don't fall off the mountain.' As usual, his comment contained more than a reference to the physical world.

Bangkok was our first stop. It was the first time I had ever been outside of Australia. I felt like the flight over was a significant part of my new spiritual quest. I was 32, turning 33 at the end of the tour.

We arrived at our hotel on New Year's Eve, planning to leave early in January for Nepal. On the first night, some of the others on the trek went downstairs to the bar. I didn't drink or feel particularly comfortable in bars but I decided to join them briefly. The bar was noticeably quiet. I ordered a mineral water and sat in a low chair in the dimly lit room. A woman came over and knelt before me on the floor, yet nothing was said. All around the room, female staff sat at the feet of the customers. I could sense there was something on offer there. Ken had already been proposed marriage on two occasions in the few hours since we landed. Whatever was happening here in the bar was far subtler. I had a sense that if I had said yes, assenting in any way at all, my life would be decided and I would have taken a completely different path. I finished my drink and took my leave, going back to the hotel room. It fascinated me how our choices can be so powerful at times. I had a very clear lesson in discernment that day.

I was travelling with friends and it felt divine. I had known Neri for a little over a year or two, and our other fellow traveller Ken for a few months. We got on well and the three of us shared the excitement of this wonderful time. Our joy was like that of children playing, but also of adults opening to the potentials of such a great adventure.

The light in Bangkok was different to that in Australia. It was luminous, and the sunset made the entire sky glow in warm yellow and orange colours. The glass-walled hotel across from us reflected this golden glow back upon us like an intense blessing from the setting sun. When walking in the street I would suddenly feel an urge to put my hands in prayer position and close my eyes. I couldn't help but stand there and enter into prayer. I had never felt the need to do this in Australia.

At one moment, in an inner vision, I saw a golden light-form of Buddha seated in prayer position over the entire city. The Buddha wasn't there on the physical level but was definitely there in Spirit. I was in awe of seeing this stunning numinous form, around and above me, looking back towards Australia. It felt incredibly special and exceptionally grand.

Visiting the local shops, I was taken by the sensitivity of the people I met. There was something incredibly peaceful in being in Bangkok. It was my first time in a foreign land and I was intoxicated by the experience. In fact, I was so enchanted by the energy of one of the female shopkeepers, that I purchased some sandals that didn't even fit me. So many new sensations caused a heightened state of awareness and my practical brain was on holidays. I was bubbling with joy.

I could feel a higher spirit calling me and, for a time, I went mostly within myself.

Nepal

We arrived in Nepal with a bang. The airport luggage-belt hadn't worked in decades and people who may have been employees grabbed our bags and raced off to the other end of the building.

We had no clear idea if these people were airport officials or not. When we caught up with them, the cases had been opened and the people were rummaging through our things. As a first experience in a new land, it was quite a shock.

Luggage searched, we were shown the open door. There was so much activity it felt quite daunting. A mini bus arrived to escort us to our hotel and I felt substantial relief and gratitude for that. The culture was extremely busy compared to the quietitude I was used to. The hotel was very well built and in a most peaceful location. At the evening meal I felt like I had ascended to heaven. The air was fresh, the staff regally polite, and our meals were exquisite. It was as if this place had never known stress. I felt like we were in the land of gods, and we the honoured guests.

We had a day in Kathmandu before leaving for the trek and I visited the giant stupa temple at Boudhanath. The whole structure was clad in multi-coloured prayer flags flapping in the wind, and thousands of people chanting 'Om Mani Padme Hum.' My tent mate for the tour came with me for the day to help me find a perfect set of ritual cymbals. This involved playing every cymbal we came across. We tried out hundreds, which added to the effect of all the sounds, smells, and the incredible atmosphere of this strange new land. I also tried out a Tibetan temple horn, which I wanted to buy though I knew I could never get it back home.

It was a beautiful sunny day and I stood next to some monks. My senses were heightened and I could see the stupa radiating blessings throughout the surrounding area. The monks also radiated, and I could see and feel how their work benefitted the community.

At the temple I drew my hand across the prayer wheels. I prayed that the people of the valley below would be blessed and I was taken aback to see an energy go in the direction of my prayers. All my senses were lit up and I was seeing very positive energies at play.

Wandering the streets of Kathmandu I weathered the shock of the different culture. If I looked at something a vendor was selling, I was immediately swamped by a dozen other sellers. It was all so new and fascinating, and so difficult to train myself to not look at the wares. Having lived alone for so many years, having so many people ignore my personal space was also very difficult for me. At the other end of the scale, there were times of sublime peace. I watched a painter applying his art to the outside wall of a temple. At the pace he was going, it looked as though he had been painting this one image for years, with several more years to go. It was a beautiful picture of a reclining, feminine deity. I wondered what motivated the painter to dedicate himself to such a long, and seemingly painstaking task. Then the word 'Service' appeared before me. From a western perspective, I had been used to people working ambitiously for an outcome, or for profit, or just to beat time, but here was a man whose quiet-moving life was in service to a greater cause.

His painting was his medium of devotion, and his efforts would contribute more to the community than just the painting itself. I could sense around me how many people here lived similarly, in efforts that acted like prayer. Each action in this state of mind gave much to a culture of peace.

In my room at the Hotel the night before the trek, I opened the bedside table to find a Bible. Holding the Bible I asked: 'What is there here that is relevant for me now?' At random I opened the book and pointed. Where my finger touched the page I read: 'Exalt the Lord our God and worship at His holy mountain, for the Lord our God is holy.' (Psalm 99:9.)

I was taken aback by how relevant the quote was. It was a message from the inner worlds as I prepared myself for what was to be a very special journey.

The seats on our transport truck were fabric stretched across metal frames. The journey would go throughout the day and all through the night before we would reach the starting point for the trek. There was little comfortable about it, except for the high spirits of the bus driver and the eight or so people who sang with him throughout the night. They laughed and sang and made merry for many hours. So much celebration of life! I wondered how the driver was able to keep his focus.

Every so often we would stop, in the middle of nowhere, for roadside business. Toilet was anywhere you could find that was out of sight. Tent shops offered a glass of sweet and spicy milk tea, a treat that lives with me to this day.

The environment felt so challenging, as it was nothing like I had ever experienced before. We were in near pitch black conditions, out in the middle of who knew where. I was happy to just stay close to the truck and hold onto the likelihood that I would eventually reach my destination.

We arrived early in the morning after many hours on the road. After resting our truck-weary bodies and checking the gear, we were on our way. I'm not sure what I expected, but was surprised when people just left to begin the walk. Maybe I thought there would be a ritual of some kind. Our trek began in a field, just outside a small village that made the usual chai-like tea. Ten minutes into a four-week trek, I stopped to enjoy a cup. It felt like a very special occasion.

We left the village and made our way up the beginning of an inclining, narrow road. There was a river on my left as I walked along the base of foothills. Some local children were drawn to us and I loved listening to them laugh and speak. Their sounds and bright playful spirit struck me as richly as the views. I also delighted in seeing how much the earth displayed its riches here. All my life I had loved rocks and minerals, precious and otherwise, and here I found an entire treasury. Stones that I had only ever seen in collections were embedded underfoot and in the hillside walls.

Our trek leader had suggested that we leave our watches behind at the hotel and I had followed his advice. After walking up a gradual incline for some hours, I felt myself pass through an invisible door. It surprised me momentarily but it also made sense. This was just another of life's usually hidden realms. I walked through a doorway that I couldn't see but was able to feel, which took me into a place beyond time. I can no longer recall exact details, except to know that it happened.

That afternoon, when I tried to write a letter home, I found that it was impossible to do so. There was such an energy in simply being present in the time and place. There was no possibility of post for weeks anyway, even if I had been able to record my thoughts.

At the end of the first day trekking, I could feel that all my years of training had prepared me for only this first day. I was aware that every subsequent day would require more from me and that this would increase exponentially. These challenges would not only be physical but also mental and emotional.

Conversations were wonderful in the Nepalese countryside. So little ever happened that meetings generally centred around the weather. I could not speak Nepalese, other than to wish someone Namaste (meaning something like, 'I bow to you, and I bow to the divine that is in each of us'). I also knew the word for thank you, but was advised that this wasn't part of the culture the way it was back home.

Many locals we met along the way referred to each other as sister and brother. If someone did speak any English, the sharing was usually as simple as 'Nice day,' or 'Doesn't feel like rain.' With the sheer magnificence of nature all around us, it was natural that the weather took central focus.

When we walked on flat lands, the respite gave my mind the chance to unwind. There was little to negotiate and this allowed thoughts to arise. I recalled a lifetime of large and small adventures, as well as many day-to-day experiences. Memories of family and friends would present, and I just allowed each thought to come and go. It felt therapeutic to allow this flow of thought, rather than to ponder and construct. As I walked, my mind became a flowing stream.

That afternoon, we were informed that a local army general wanted us to be his guests. We chose to accept his hospitality and set up our camp for the night. Visiting his house we entered a building with a lounge room not much bigger than two metres square. There were seven of us trekking and he had invited all of the locals to his home as well. His generosity extended to getting us drunk on a local beverage called Raksi, which turned out to be incredibly potent. I hadn't drunk alcohol for over seven years, and the Raksi hit the mark hard. I recall getting quite loud and excited about being so drunk on the remarkable homemade brew. I also recall dancing a lot, and I was fortunate that evening not to fall off the mountain. No one mentioned anything the next day, so I can only hope that my behaviour wasn't offensive to anyone.

We had been trekking for about a week and I had adjusted to feeling worn out and exhausted most of the time. At the end of an extremely long and stress-filled day, we arrived at a hut at the top of a mountain range, which was a great relief after trekking through heavy snow. It was late afternoon, going on to early evening. The light was starting to fade and the temperature was dropping fast. For the briefest of moments, it was an enormous relief just to have found shelter.

As soon as we had gathered to light the fire, a large group of Sherpas piled into the small space as well. The relative security and momentary peace became an experience of intense claustrophobia for me. The Sherpas began removing timber boards from off the walls of the hut to feed the fire. Freezing night air was rushing in and I wanted to scream. We were all quite cold and it disturbed me that they were destroying our place of shelter for the night. In exhaustion and to maintain my sanity, I pushed my way to the earthen floor. I needed to find myself space where I felt that I could breathe. I put my face close to the cold earth and gave myself a serious talking to: I could cope with this. I had to cope with this.

Thankfully someone began yelling orders and the Sherpas stopped tearing the boards from the wall. They also soon left us there and found themselves a second hut a little further down the way. There was an overhang on our hut and we pitched our tents under that. I got into my sleeping bag as soon as I could. I had survived an intense bout of stress. It gave me comfort that I had been able to deal with more stress than I thought possible. It had been a crushing feeling but I had been able to find a sense of inner peace beyond it all. The exhaustion of the day now called for sleep.

We were high up in the mountains and in the morning when I opened the tent flap, I went into near ecstasy. We were above the level of the clouds. A blanket of brilliant white cloud stretched out before our feet. I felt like I was on the top of the world, and I was.

Prayer

Many times along the trail, I felt that I should stop and place my hands in prayer position in front of my heart. It was becoming a very pleasant practice for me. I was in such a sacred place and wanted to acknowledge it. It also felt like an alignment to the truest aspect of myself. I felt free to behave in the way that was right and holy for me.

At different times we had to wade across near freezing rivers. The water was icy cold, and fortunately we had the gear needed to get us through. Sometimes I just had to stop in the middle of the river and acknowledge the spirit of place with reverence. The physical aspect of the river certainly required great respect also. There was no point in drowning just because I had found nirvana.

Throughout the trek I often walked at a different pace to the others. Some days I would try to keep up but other times I preferred to walk more slowly and take in the sights. One day I could hardly believe my eyes. Before me was a waterfall as tall an eight story building – frozen. Then I noticed that the entire area was the same, with every waterfall frozen in space. Even the splash at the base of each waterfall was fixed like an ice sculpture. It was an extraordinary natural wonderland and it took my breath away. Whatever efforts and difficulties I had been through, it was more than worth it. I was in one of the most magical places on Earth.

We came to an area where we had to walk around a deep crevasse. The only path around the mountains was about fifty centimetres wide. To survive this part of the walk required complete concentration for the next hour or more. I had already learned on the flat tracks that if you look away from the direction you're walking, it is almost certain that you will veer off the path. Now my life depended on keeping eyes straight ahead and taking supreme care with every step. Much of the path was also covered in ice. I developed some very clear mind-body focus on this trek.

Every day brought new challenges. It was hard to believe the height of some of the mountains we had to climb. Hours later, looking back, it was difficult to believe just how far we had come. Every day I was surprised by what I was capable of accomplishing and I imagine the others felt the same.

Many days the weather was so cold that I had to dance on the spot while the Sherpas cooked our meal. It didn't help that they began each meal's preparation by heating the snow in order to clean the pots. They were very methodical in how they did things. Some days the preparation alone could take an hour, which meant walking up and down on the spot so my toes didn't freeze. Then I would have to continue my dancing while eating the food. There was no other option than to keep moving.

The cold was uncomfortable but we were surrounded by nature's beauty everywhere. Every now and then I would find a single wildflower, rare and resilient, showing itself through the snow. Nearly everything was covered in hoar frost crystals, brilliant white, crisp formations on dormant shrubs and bare trees. Some days I walked through native rhododendron forests. Other times we traveled paths where the snow was two metres high on each side of us.

One day, while walking alone in the high mountains, I came across some giant rocks by a river. These were large pieces of a mountain that had broken away and found their homes by the water. Sitting down to rest, I was quite surprised when I experienced the rocks imparting their counsel to me. It was a most blessed occasion, and yet another stretch of my consciousness to take it all in.

Healing

After walking for over three weeks, we were now deep into the Sagamartha National Park, not far from the glacier, and ready for our final push up to Gokyo Peak. I woke feeling ill, only able to manage to walk for four or five minutes at a time. No sooner had I recovered enough to walk, that I collapsed to the ground again. My face felt supported in contact with the snow and my Sherpa carers sat patiently with me at each fall. There was nothing I could do except lie there and wait for my energy to return.

It took about fifteen minutes to regain the strength to stand and walk and within minutes I would feel ill and fall again. In one hour I had covered less than fifty metres and couldn't see how I could go on. We were weeks into the mountain range and my mind began to contemplate how I might be transported out. The Sherpas were incredibly supportive and were laughing and joking while they waited for me to recover. It helped that they had such positive cheerfulness and weren't overly concerned about the situation.

My main lesson that day was in being able to go past my ego. I felt freed from having to project dignity or manliness. I had no choice but to let go of these pretences. I was as pathetic as I had ever been, yet being in this condition gave me a mental strength. I had been useless but nobody seemed to mind. The illness passed after a few hours, and I was able to catch up with the group by nightfall.

There were several experiences like this that broke me down so that I went beyond worrying. Indeed, one of the best benefits of trekking in Nepal was to break through various fears and find an appreciation of life independent of circumstances.

Other days just brought fun. One day, lost in a blizzard, we made small snow-figures while we waited hours for our guides to find our hidden tracks. We had no idea if they would even be able to find those paths, so we had to put our minds to something else. On another occasion, the sun was out and there was a brilliant light. When I looked up, I saw many Sherpas running up a moderate mountain slope, only so they could then slide down it again. There was such an elated feeling in the group that day, as people played on the mountain slide.

When we finally reached the apex of Gokyo Ri, there was an incredible sense of accomplishment. I had completed the task I set myself. I had survived an inspiring ordeal. There was such a sense of relief as well as of deep inner peace. Our guides were excited and taking celebratory photos of each other and the group. I felt a sense of unity within myself and with the mountain. From our mountain, I could look across at Sagamartha with great awe and appreciation. It was so beautiful standing there and the sense of completion was incomparable.

In an elated state, without any advanced thinking, I sat on my raincoat and slid down the steep side of Gokyo peak. About half way down, when I had picked up quite a speed, my backside hit a rock. It hit incredibly hard and I thought I had broken the base of my spine. The pain was intense and I wondered how I would get to a hospital. It was one of the most stupid things I had done in my life. I was very relieved when the pain finally subsided and I found out I could still walk.

We trekked for several more days to get through to Lukla where we could fly back to Kathmandu. Despite having booked tickets, there was no guarantee of a flight out. Fortunately our tour company knew someone at the air services, whose relative owned the local hotel. We payed for an open bar for the town that night and, in return we were guaranteed our flights. It was an effective way of getting things done. It was not really a bribe but an exchange of favours.

It was my 33rd birthday, and I spent it on the mountain in Lukla, as the only sober person in the town. I was alone, listening to the reveling around me, with a quiet sense of connection to spirit. I was at peace and happy. I had climbed a mountain.

It was a welcome thing to connect with civilisation again, after four weeks of experiencing all manner of effort and difficulties, as well as inspirations. It had been the most uplifting and profound time of my life, and I had never felt so worn out.

The hot water at the hotel wasn't working, and we sat as a group in deckchairs in the afternoon sun. I had never felt so satisfied with myself before. The mountains and the journey had meant a lot to me, as did the relaxation that followed. I had experienced illness, pain, fears, as well as emotional and physical exhaustion. I had been to the edges of my abilities in many ways and now I basked in a near ecstatic glory. I was dirty and my hair stood on end. I had also grown a beard after it became too painful to shave at minus 20 degrees Celsius. The hot water came back on in the late afternoon and I took my time returning to the modern world.

Descending the Mountain

Back home in Australia, I was now aware of the prayer: 'not my will but Thy Will be done.' I wanted for higher-consciousness to come into my life. I had come to believe that my personal wishes would probably only prolong my earthly sufferings. I was ready to surrender my will to the Divine and see what life would present. After such a rare experience, I was conscious how much I had been changed by the journey.

I felt compelled to put my life in order. I cleaned and ordered every cupboard. It was unlike me to be bursting with vitality, but I took to swimming lengths of a local pool each day. I also increased my voluntary work, offering my services to many local church and charity organisations. I had been to the mountaintop and now had to adjust to life in the flat lands of Melbourne. It wasn't too long before my energies started to settle down again and my body adjusted to the thicker air and suburban mindset. After two weeks I finally had all the feeling back in each of my toes. It had been so cold. I celebrated having avoided frostbite.

Courting Shy

Back at my classes at Augustine, I had an experience that reawakened my deep grief at losing Angie eight years before. I had become attracted to a woman there and begun a hesitant relationship. The hesitation was on her side and, after a few frustrating months, she ended the relationship. When my grief was triggered and reawakened, I knew I needed help. I heard of a spiritual healer named Cheryl, and I felt comfortable to seek her professional support. There was another sign from the universe that it was time to move on. One evening at the Augustine Centre, on winning the door prize, I was given a small door.

Everyone else had a good laugh, and I was left standing there holding this 'prize'. It struck me that I had not only been given a door, I had been 'shown the door' as well. This presented me with the idea that it was time to start a new chapter.

05 - Seeking True North

Meeting Cheryl was to take me into worlds even more interesting than I had already traversed. At first she seemed like an average Australian woman but she was quite extraordinary. Within a short time I came to see her as my doorway to higher consciousness.

Cheryl worked at a medical healing centre not far from where I lived. I arrived early and sat quietly in the waiting room. I needed a lot of healing and hoped that Cheryl could help me do this. I had heard of a technique called rebirthing and hoped that this might reconnect me with myself. I was primed for a whole new entry into life.

Cheryl arrived and I was pleasantly surprised. She was a bright young woman, with intense eyes, and her own way of dressing. Her blonde hair was long and somewhat wild, and she wore a loose woollen jumper with patches. Her legs sported blotchy-inked leg-tights, and tall green leather boots. Cheryl shared that she had just returned from a few days staying at an ocean beach with her dog Camilla. I learned that Cheryl enjoyed swimming in waterfalls, and this reflected in her hair, which still looked damp and unbrushed. There was something about her that was radiant and other-worldly.

Cheryl was happy to consider doing rebirthing with me, but our first session would be a spiritual healing and an appraisal. She explained the healing process and I shared with her why I had come. Cheryl needed to ascertain my level of balance and readiness for the rebirthing work. At the beginning of the healing session, I heard her saying some prayers, asking that I be given help. During the healing, I could see how my last partner and I had been joined at our feet. I then watched a vision of how we were separated, as if by surgery of light. Suddenly I felt free from her, and the pain I had been experiencing the past week or more was gone. It was such grace to be so liberated in just one healing session.

I made another appointment and left with a new skill for separating myself from old relationships. It became an immediate habit to say prayers and ask for inner help. I became aware of how much unfinished business I had been carrying and how effective the healing work was in releasing this. Most old relationships seemed like simple separations but in some I noticed the negative ties were as thick as tree trunks. When any emotional pain about my last partner tried to return, I learnt to breathe through my mouth and the emotions were bypassed. I also used this to manage many other transitions.

I became aware that by bringing my grief about the separation home with me, I had created a place for this sadness to sit, right in my doorway. Each evening when I went home, I was walking into the thought-forms and took to believing them again. Cheryl taught me some simple techniques for dispelling these energies and cleansing my home. By making conscious what I had been unconsciously creating, and by asking for angelic help, I was able to clear away many old energies and experienced great relief.

At the end of my next healing session, Cheryl relayed an important question to me: 'Man choose, dark or light. Man choose.' This was confronting, as I assumed that I already lived in the light. Cheryl repeated the challenge. On reflection, I could see that I had lived in shadows for many years. I decided that there was a choice to make and I happily made it. I grasped the opportunity. I had no idea how much grace would be given or how much more healing work would have to be done, but at least now I was conscious of a doorway to the Light. I wanted to be healed and to live in the Light.

In Cheryl, I had met someone with whom I felt a deep camaraderie. Finally, I had found a person who was on a similar wavelength to me. I could feel that she genuinely cared for humanity as a whole. There was the potential for us to be close friends.

It was time for me to make a significant decision. Cheryl was about to start regular classes teaching spiritual healing, and these were on the same night as my soul dance sessions. I had been participating in movement-dance classes every week for three years. It had been the heart of my creative expression. I dearly wanted to continue but I needed to take up the training with Cheryl. It was such a difficult decision to make, but I had to move on. I met with my dance teacher Tony, and informed him of my decision. It had been a wonderful relationship learning from him, and I had gone through so much growth under his guidance and care. It was a pretty ordinary moment for me, telling him that I was going to leave.

I filled in the enrolment form for Cheryl's spiritual healing course, and went to the letterbox to post it. The simple action of putting the letter in the mailbox felt almost impossible. I had made the decision, but now met with added resistance. I tried several times but was confronted by an almost physical resistance to my posting it. I circled the letterbox for at least ten minutes, and finally made the commitment. At that very moment of posting the letter, I felt like a huge invisible crane picked me up high into the air, and then placed me down in another part of the universe. It was a large, inner shift. What I thought was just moving on in my training, was actually a complete change of life direction.

On the first night of the healing course, I could feel how the energy centres in my body (chakras) were out of alignment. Attending the course helped me become much more clear about how to cleanse and align these inner bodies. An entire new level of my education had begun.

In another healing, I saw what was almost certainly a past life. Cheryl was playing music that was Native American in essence, and it stirred something within my very soul. In vision, I saw myself hanging with a hook through my chest. On lifting my head and opening my physical eyes, I saw that the ends of my trousers were from this native time. They were frayed like those of a Native American man, and I was wearing moccasins. I was aware that something had occurred at that time, requiring much healing. After the session, Cheryl relayed how she had also seen that I had been connected to a medicine man and had healing to do from that time. The spirituality of the Native American life was something that Cheryl and I shared very closely. Both of us had been deeply affected by what we had endured back then. Twenty-five years after this healing, I found out that I had been tortured by another tribe. They had done this in order to break the young men before they became full warriors. Some healing takes many years. Indeed, it can take lifetimes.

For a time I found that I was awakened to giving healings and I began invoking a lot of prayers for others. A couple of weeks later that energy closed down again. I needed to go through a process first. It would take several years to prepare myself to be a spiritual healer. First, I would need to cleanse and purify

94

my inner bodies, developing understanding and right intention. I had sustained damage from my many years in the wilderness and my youthful excesses. I had to close down to certain lower energies, and develop a stronger, cleaner aura. I was awakening to higher vibrations, and needed to approach my training like any other profession, in a serious and methodical way.

One of my first experiences of the degree of Cheryl's knowledge and connection with the spiritual, was when I felt seriously uneasy at home one day. I felt like I was being psychically attacked and phoned Cheryl for her help. She told me about Archangel Michael and about calling on his protection. Cheryl suggested that we would both call on this great angelic Light. When I got off the phone and did as she had suggested I saw a deep blue light surround my entire body. I immediately felt safe and free from what had been disturbing me. It was such a clear experience of receiving help from the inner levels.

Rebirthing

I had a plan with Cheryl, that we would soon begin dry rebirthing, and gradually build up to having sessions in a hot tub. In the meantime I went to see another psychologist who was also known for doing this work. His name was Graham and he had a practice on the outskirts of the city. When I arrived at his rooms I noticed a framed photograph, on his entrance wall, of the spiritual teacher Sai Baba. Looking at the picture in the hallway, I saw a rainbow appear. This colourful light appeared out of nothing and went the small distance across the hall, onto the image. I could not give any explanation for the phenomenon. It gave me confidence that I was in the right place.

Graham appeared and invited me into his practice room. The room wasn't large, and was made smaller by the large blocks of foam covering every surface. Walls, floor and ceiling were all made of thick, rubbery foam that was covered in a womb-like red coloured material. It was about one metre thick on the floor and difficult to walk on. Graham invited me to relax and talk to him briefly. Within a minute of beginning, he placed his hands each side of my face and gently held my head. Without warning, I found that I had lost contact with my normal consciousness, and was now in the middle of being born. My head was crowning and I was deep within the birthing process. The intensity of the experience was surprising, and very real. My day-to-day mindset had surrendered to going deep into the process. Graham gently manipulated my head, like that of a doctor, pulling a newborn free. At the conclusion of the session I felt very refreshed, and I was astonished by what had just occurred. It was such a big shift in a matter of moments. Graham was a psychologist who worked regularly with Sai Baba in India, and a healer with powerful forces behind him.

Cheryl identified the patterns I held from a forceps birth and planned a series of sessions where we would work on this. She taught me the continuous breathing patterns that stimulated reconnecting with birth and, after practising these, we organised a hot tub. The tub was heated to the temperature of the womb at the time of birth. The breathing and the water made me feel comfortable about relinquishing control. My nose had a clip on it, to prevent breathing in any water, and the mouth was sealed using a snorkel to breath in air. Cheryl supported my body so that I could completely let go, and the breathing technique soon took me into a womb like place. My hands went into tetany, where my fingers curled up like those of a foetus', though I remained conscious of Cheryl's instructions throughout.

We worked on how the forceps birth had affected me and the associated patterns. At an unconscious level, I feared to ask for help. My psyche held the belief that asking for help would mean suffering pain. I knew that I was in a shallow hot tub with a healer but for the life of me, I couldn't bring myself to just stand up. I was in great distress reliving the moments of the intervention but unable to help myself. Cheryl supported me as best she could and sent healing energies to the obvious trauma. I thrashed about for at least five minutes and was exhausted by it. At the end of the session, more clear minded, I lay on the grass in the sunshine for half an hour, unable to move. I could hear the concerned owner of the tub, questioning Cheryl on what she had done to me. Cheryl, being quite sensitive and clairvoyant, was confident, allowing the process to take its course.

When I finally felt able to dress and get into her car, I sat like a baby, with a giant grin on my face, all the way home. I was in a newborn's consciousness, in a state of pure bliss. I felt wonderful.

At the end of my next spiritual healing session, as I prepared to leave, a vision came of throwing myself to my knees to propose to Cheryl. I had avoided even the idea of marriage for my thirty-three years, and didn't know what to make of this. As the impression to propose increased, I physically dug my heels into the floor to avoid any chance of kneeling. It was a very odd experience being pushed by a force that I didn't understand. I successfully resisted but then asked if Cheryl had time or interest to meet with me socially. Cheryl got out her diary as if she was booking another healing session and there was a pause as she considered my request. Cheryl declared that she had an hour available the following week and we could meet at a nearby parkland. We also made an appointment for another healing.

At the park, we walked and shared. I broached with Cheryl the possibility of getting to know her better. She was interested but also crystal clear that she already had a commitment to support the work of her spiritual teacher. She could only consider dating me if I also felt resonance with this person. I had no idea who Cheryl's teacher was, but I was willing to find out.

At Cheryl's suggestion, I would attend an Earth Healing Service that her teacher was facilitating. I was beginning to meet some other people who were part of this work, and they seemed to be especially good-hearted. That Sunday, the service was focused on Divine Truth and I had a very positive response to it. The program included prayers, invocations, positive affirmations, meditation and singing. I found it to be very uplifting. I was surprised at how much it was in alignment with what I had already been studying over the preceding years.

In the meditation during the service, I had another clear inner vision: my life path and Cheryl's were parallel. This vision of railway-like lines stretched forever into the distance was clear and fascinating. I was getting used to my intuition providing information via visions and insights.

On the following Sunday the service was conducted by Cheryl's teacher, Ananda. I was a little on edge not knowing what to expect, but also quite interested in how my world was expanding. When it came time for the meditation, Ananda had chosen the music by Oliver Shanti called *Licht Prakash Light*, and on hearing it, I was immediately transported into the bliss I experienced in Nepal. It was the exact same music that I had purchased in Kathmandu on the last day of my journey there. Between the energy created within the service and the spirit I had experienced in the mountains, I became aware of a bridge between the Himalayas and Australia in that moment.

At the next service I was presented with yet another vision of Cheryl, in a wedding dress, as my bride. I found this to be quite confronting and tried to turn my head away. I had avoided marriage for most of my life, but recently had felt open to the possibility. I had been invoking as my truth that I was 'in the perfect relationship for me now,' and my prayer was being answered. In Cheryl, I had met my complement.

Cheryl nourished me physically as well as spiritually. My enjoyment of her company became stronger as we shared our hopes and dreams with each other. I felt within me that we had a commitment from another time, like a promise that was being recommissioned. While I heard a voice from my childhood declaring, 'When in doubt, don't', I proposed anyway. I had to act on what I felt to be right before it could be clouded by fears. Cheryl said yes.

It was time to meet Cheryl's teacher, who was interested in meeting me. As I lay down to sleep that night, I became aware that Ananda was present in spirit, standing at the end of the bed. With an easy trust I welcomed her to look into me all she liked. This teacher could see more about me than I knew about myself. After this, we met personally, and I felt very graced. Ananda was the most loving, bright light. Full of love and humour, radiating joy. I felt very welcome and at ease. Ananda also had a serious side to her, to which I gave full respect. I felt a blessed affinity with this gracious spiritual teacher.

I began attending many of the activities, enjoying the love and joy that was present in Ananda's work. Ananda also held evensong at her home and workshops on important topics related to walking a spiritual path. She would cover how to manage one's psychological traits and maintain balance as one progresses along the Path. Spiritual Psychology was also Cheryl's field and the main focus of my own studies over the past ten years.

The Usual Unusual Events

One afternoon, meditating at Cheryl's place, I called on a higher aspect of myself, my *I Am Presence*, to send into me a white cleansing flame. To my very pleasant surprise, I experienced a profound inner vision where the entire room became ablaze with this Light. It felt like I was on fire and being purified by this brilliant white flame. The inner help had been well and truly turned up.

Memories started leaving my being. I could feel them as if they were physical as they were released from my body. This became so intense that I was concerned at how well I might function at the end of the strange experience. I was worried how much consciousness I would have left. My only explanation for the intensity of this experience was that it was probably related to my decision to work for the Light with Cheryl. My inner structure was being altered for the work to come. I had the sense in this meditation that whomever she chose as her partner would be given this added stimulus. I had no clear idea of what lay ahead except that it was probably going to be quite a ride.

Learning to Share

When I decided to move in with Cheryl, I let go of my past. I put most of what I had owned into charity donation bins and felt immediately free. I only kept some clothes and work tools but let go of nearly everything else. I was ready to begin an entirely new life.

Living and working with Cheryl, I quickly learned about serving and walking a path of renunciation. This did not mean having to go without, but to live in a state of non-attachment. The initial lessons came through living in a shared house. This certainly wasn't easy for me, as apart from the brief but wonderful flow of gypsy life in Tasmania, I had been living alone or in my own space for well over a decade. Being with others and making contributions was a pleasure but I struggled to find balance. I found myself doing most of the food preparation but being left with nothing by the time I sat down at the table. The others had eaten most of the food in a rush. I was used to taking my time in creating a meal, then contemplating where the food had come from, and giving thanks before eating. Now in a household where many others would eat together, I quickly learned that if I didn't change my ways I would entirely miss out.

I also noticed how some people helped themselves to whatever was in the pantry, but never replaced the items. I took to storing my food in Cheryl's clothes cupboard so I could be assured of having something to eat when I got home. There were many adjustments to make to shared living arrangements, and it often felt like a bit of a mad house. People were using my things without respecting them the way I would have and this put me under a lot of stress.

With my spiritual development so rapid, it took a lot for my personality to adjust. Over the years I had already experienced a kind of death at least a couple of times but in working with Cheryl, I was being asked to give much more. She found so many ways to engage me in the work, challenging many of my fears. I also discovered anger and fury that I now had to manage. All my buttons were being pressed at once. Cheryl was teaching me about unconditional love, and I had to let go of many of my past ways of seeing the world. I was learning that love is what you give without any expectation of return or reward. Either you give love freely, or you aren't really loving at all.

This was a new concept for me and my personality took a while to get used to it. I would give and give and give, as it gave me much pleasure to do so. But then, when people seemed to just take and not give back, I would find myself disturbed. Over time I learned to give only what I wished to give freely, and I found a joy and a balance in that. I found that any divergence from this simply created suffering. I found it difficult for a time because of ingrained patterns and unconscious beliefs, but I could feel it was the path I wanted to take.

Another of my new tutors was Cheryl's dog Camilla. A man had mistreated Camie when she was a puppy, so I took over feeding her in order to help her learn to trust men again. Camie was a saluki and very sensitive to energies. I tried teaching her to sit and she would simply ignore me. If I wanted her to respond I had to ask her nicely and then allow her to choose. She refused to relate with me on any other terms. With Camilla, it always needed to be a request, and she always needed complete freedom in when and how she responded.

In meeting Cheryl I had gone from doing occasional voluntary activities to working pretty much seven days and nights each week. Cheryl was driven to serve the welfare of others and I wanted to support her. I felt a deep affinity with the work she was doing and it became my full-time job. My previous decade of withdrawal and investigation quickly shifted to a life in service. At thirty-three years of age I had finally found the gold at the end of the rainbow. I had found true love, my co-worker and a worthy cause. I had connected with meaning and purpose in life.

Cheryl offered sessions in psychotherapy, counselling, spiritual healing, guided imagery, regression and crystal work. She also taught workshops so that her clients could learn to better help themselves. I took on the administration and marketing so as to support her in broadening this work.

One evening when we were meditating together, Cheryl came out of her peace with a jolt. She had seen something that frightened her. A friend consoled her and after a short time we began again. Afterwards she explained that she had seen us in a previous life, where we had been men who met daily, possibly in England. We had met on a park bench at lunchtimes, for shared conversation, for many years. She had seen that one day one of us didn't appear because that person had died. When she went back into the meditation, she was shown images of clocks, and an inner voice reassuring her that in this life we would have 'enough time.' I thought no more of it, but it turned out to be significant.

Karma Yoga

Ananda was teaching those who were attracted to her, to work with the principles of right human relations: To steer one's actions by the principles of love, truth, unselfishness, and with purity of heart. It was a pleasure to be around such a person and be uplifted by her presence. For most of my life I had rejected authority, but in Ananda I felt a true authority. She was love personified and I was greatly inspired by that. I gladly volunteered some of my spare time to help out in various activities.

My first task at the ashram was the cleaning of rubbish bins. They were almost as big as I was, and I would wash them clean once a week. I was not used such activities but I found some joy in this. It was the perfect task for me to begin this new level of my spiritual path; cleaning bins equated with cleansing my ego and allowing in more soul light. Over time I would learn the joy of selfless service, no matter what the tasks.

Time was my own and I volunteered for many duties, including cleaning offices, bathrooms, toilets and bedrooms. On Friday afternoons I helped prepare the evening meals and washed dishes afterwards. On two occasions I was put in charge of co-coordinating large festivals, as well as some tasks involving overseas travel. After several months organising and co-coordinating one of the festivals, I felt at the top of my game. I had held a major role, in creating a day where many spiritual and new age groups came together to share their teachings and practices. I developed work outlines, lecture schedules, equipment hire, and co-coordinated with the many different attending groups. I felt alive in my new role, finding out just how many skills and abilities I had. The week after the festival had been completed, I was back in charge of cleaning toilets. This was a perfect way to keep my ego in check.

Working for a cause meant that my shadow nature would have light shone upon it. Giving honorary service showed up many aspects that were dormant within my unconscious. Each of the tasks was perfect in helping me let go of earthly attachments and open to the joy of my soul. I found that the joy was in surrender. I was letting go of my lower nature and opening to higher-level experiences.

Blavatsky's Doorsteps

One day, while sweeping around the doorway to the ashram, I heard a voice within my head say: 'this is just like sweeping Blavatsky's doorway.' I had no idea what that meant but found that it referred to H. P. Blavatsky who co-founded the Theosophical Society with Henry Steele Olcott in 1875. I had a sense that I had an incarnation as a young Indian man at The T. S. headquarters in Adyar, and had probably swept the stairs there as well. I enjoyed sensing possible connections to different lineages. Perhaps this was a message from another humble lifetime from my past.

Cheryl and I thought about getting married later in the year. I had just enough money in the bank to cover our travel expenses, so I suggested we have a holiday in Bali. Life had been so hectic since we met that it would be good to take some time out. However, Kuta Beach was busy and it was difficult to relax. Everyone seemed to have something they wanted to sell us. I was happier going for short walks and seeing the exotic nature of the local flora. In the afternoons we relaxed by the hotel pool, and went into sublime states meditating together in our room.

I still had a lot within me to sort out and Cheryl was very kind to listen. We spent much of the week just sharing what was happening in our dreams and considering their meanings. Our time together in Bali was incredibly healing. It was the perfect opportunity to get to know each other better.

It was in Bali that I found joy in meditating daily. It was an ecstasy in spirit. On my honeymoon, in the laid-back environment of the island and its warm supportive weather, I found divinity within. That rare time imprinted my connection with joy and spirit. I was in the company of the love of my life, and happier than I had ever felt before.

It was fortunate that we had our main honeymoon before our wedding because there was little time afterwards. Cheryl and I had a spiritual wedding in October 1989 and dedicated our marriage to serving love in the world. The date for the wedding was chosen after consulting with an astrologer about which day was most auspicious for such a focus.

We set our intention, and our work over the next ten years would be relentless, as well as satisfying and fun. Most nights we would work until early in the morning on one project or another. We travelled often, as well as offering many free public lectures, paid workshops, short courses with other teachers, and we also took part in many voluntary activities. Cheryl worked seven days a week and I did my best to keep up with her. It was wonderful to be so engaged in life again and working in a way that had meaning for me. If I hadn't been young this level of work would never have been possible.

The main pressures of my new life included leaving behind a set of beliefs that related mainly to materialistic values. Now I had to embrace an unknown paradigm, where matters were more subtle and nuanced. My learning curve was more like a learning mountain!

Discernment

Jesus of Nazareth is attributed with having said: 'Be in the world, but not of it.' This was perfect guidance for me as I sought to understand this new world of spirit. In my younger days I had certainly become far too immersed in earthly pleasures, at the expense of discernment. Now I had to learn about a whole new way.

I soon understood the value of being cautious, when making decisions on a spiritual path. To succeed, I would have to be willing to allow wisdom to develop in its own time and be kind to myself when I chose poorly. I was at the gateway of a whole new world and the rules were quite difficult to assess at times. In a school of higher wisdom there were bound to be tests along the way. The tests would not be academic. They would present opportunities to see my unconscious programs. Early on, I made a choice that I believed was made in integrity, but in doing so I missed the higher principle. I had based my decision on looking after myself, but the greater lesson was in learning to be compassionate with others.

There was an energy that came with this lesson, and it shocked my nervous system. I experienced a release of great anger as well as a desire to argue in my defence. I threw cooking pots at the kitchen wall and smashed my entire music collection on the floor. Things that had been generally annoying to me suddenly became volcanic. Cheryl, who had delivered the message, waited while I vented my stress. Moments later I could feel that I simply needed to accept the teaching and continue to open to the higher principles. This would require me to be transformed. It would not be easy but I reaffirmed my commitment to learn all I could, and make whatever efforts it would take.

The lesson also cost Cheryl and I much closeness in our relationship as she had to take on the role of teacher in relaying this lesson to me. Cheryl was used as a vehicle that carried the energy of higher will, striking and shaking old programs within me. Neither of us was happy about it but we understood that this was part of the course we had chosen to take. To serve to the best of our ability would involve various lessons and sacrifices along the way.

It is easy to convince oneself that an old way of thinking is good enough but the spiritual path requires serious contemplation and reassessment of what the path really is. Old habits die hard, especially as the ego clings to them for identification and a sense of security. I console myself that I can only ever do my best and that has to be enough. At the end of the day after all, God is Love.

Travels

By Christmas we were ready to travel again. The organisation we were a part of was going on a Peace Tour to Israel, Egypt and Greece. There were nearly 200 people attending, coming from all over the world.

In Israel I found the beauty of history as well as place. I had briefly studied the Bible in school days, and here I was in the middle of everything I had read about. I could imagine where Jesus had walked and see the places where he had been. We travelled through deserts where Bible texts had been hidden in caves and took some time out to float on the Dead Sea with the fortress of Masada just across the way. So many members of my spiritual family were around me that day. There was such great joy as friends covered themselves in the therapeutic mud and floated in the salty sea.

Jerusalem was a strange blend. There was much conflict in the air and tension at various venues. I met anger in some of the young men who carried high-tech weapons but I also experienced a sublime beauty in the land where Jesus had lived and taught. It was powerful to sit in the garden of Gethsemane and wander through the streets of Jerusalem, Bethany and Bethlehem.

Before we left on this journey, during a healing, I had seen myself fall from the top of a pyramid. When I asked the image what it was trying to tell me, the words came: 'fell from grace.' This hit hard and was quite confronting. Now that I was in Egypt, several unusual experiences were set to unfold.

Lying down in my hotel room, I found it almost impossible to move. Something was containing me, as though I was wrapped and encased like a mummy. I was becoming quite claustrophobic and Cheryl offered me some help. During the healing she began hand movements, as if she was unwrapping bandages that were there from a previous time. Whatever the truth of it was, I certainly felt relieved at the conclusion of the healing.

Later in the week, we visited the Great Pyramid at Giza. We had walked around the base of the structure to see the museum at its rear. On our return to the front, I experienced an entity come out from the enormous stone structure and embed itself in my body. I wrestled with it for a while, and then felt that I would just allow it to be. I had no idea what was going on but I felt to trust the experience. On returning to the front face of the pyramid, whatever it was - spirit or trapped soul - it just left my body and I never felt it again. I was never sure of its relationship to me but I knew that something had been trapped inside the pyramid and took its freedom through me that day. Whatever it was, there had been a positive release. The world of spirit continued to amaze me.

There was nothing like being in the desert on such a rare and wonderful journey. There were many aspects of this tour that felt like being held in heaven. At other times it was a different experience.

Leaving Luxor, we were on a medium sized plane, when I felt like my skull was going to explode. For half an hour I felt the pain increasing, and honestly thought my skull might crack and that I could die. I didn't want to disturb the flight but kept wondering if the cabin pressures were wrong. The pain was almost unbearable and when it finally released, I cried with great relief. At that moment, as I looked across the aisle at friends, I could feel compassion. From out of the intense pain, I now had direct knowing of what compassion was. The pain had been part of opening me to a new level of consciousness. I viewed the process as a gift given from spirit. Possibly something my teacher had initiated.

At the end of the tour, Cheryl and I took the opportunity to fly to England. Cheryl wanted to spend some time in London and go to some places of significance to her, including participating in a meditation at the Theosophical Society Headquarters in London. The only thing in my heart was to visit the Royal Botanic Gardens at Kew. The moment I stepped through the gates, my eyes flooded with tears. I had no idea why, but I cried fully and deeply until my heart found ease. Plants had been so important to my healing ever since my breakdown, as well as being a keen interest of mine since I was a child. I was in my element that day.

This peace was turned on its head when we visited buildings associated with Henry VIII. Neither of us knew why but Cheryl and I found ourselves in some very heavy mental battles, arguing about nothing in particular. Cheryl felt that she had an incarnation in the family of Sir Thomas More and I wondered if I had been in the service of the king. Perhaps we had been on opposite sides of the court during those times. We narrowly survived some very serious arguments and had to work hard at coming back into our hearts. This we would do in Scotland at Findhorn.

Findhorn was famous for its angels and I had always wanted to visit. We arrived unannounced and spent the day trying to find someone in the community we could meet with. It was winter and the regular activities weren't running at that time of the year. Our first experience was nothing like we had expected. Virtually everyone told us to go away and come back in season.

Unable to find anyone we could speak with, we visited the community hall and marvelled at what had been created there. Wandering the streets we finally met someone who ran a bed and breakfast, and we settled in to stay the night. All night I felt a strong presence of the angels surrounding us, all happy that we were visiting.

The next day Cheryl wanted to visit various places around the area, to be a vehicle for spirit. At each she did some energy work invoking various prayers. Before we left Findhorn we purchased a board game called *The Transformation Game*. This game was designed so that players had opportunities to speak openly and honestly about important personal issues. While one spoke, the other listened. This was a breakthrough in our relationship, as it offered us a structure for sharing about important issues. It was a brilliant gift for our relatively new relationship. It also helped to heal some of our recent heavy battles in English territory.

On our return to England we drove through the central marshes and realised that we had gone past an area that Cheryl felt drawn to visiting. It was over two hours drive back through the fine rain, in the dark and on small roads, but Cheryl insisted that it was important to her. We drove through the night until we came to a field on a back-road.

We were in the countryside of Scotland, and Cheryl wanted to stop and pray at that spot. We entered the field and tried a few times to light a candle. Cheryl did her usual practice of asking for the help of spirit, invoking specific energies and saying healing prayers. It was at this point that my visions presented. The field looked strewn with dead horses in the aftermath of a war. All around us lay the results of a fierce battle from olden times. Cheryl sensed it was a battle we had both been part of, which was why we had been called there to do some healing. There was no denying what I saw. We prayed together, standing in the open field. Returning to our car, the headlights on my face stimulated another vision. I could see chain-mail that covered my head and draped over my shoulders. Who knows what we had been up to. Hopefully our present day efforts had helped to heal whatever harm had been perpetrated.

The Language of the Heart

Back in Australia, Cheryl saw in meditation that she had been given a new name. She had been shown that her true name was Tara, and not Cheryl. I could see that it fitted her well, and within the week, where Cheryl had been, Tara now stood. She also envisioned changing her surname to *Govinda-Rose*. *Govinda* represented the Buddha, and *Rose* was a symbol for Christ. The new surname, she said, represented a bridge between the Buddha and the Christ.

We had been trying to work out how we could amalgamate our surnames, but our attempts had received some derision from some friends and other people. Here was a potential name that we could both share. I had some misgivings about letting go of my family name, but I also felt that it was important in aligning myself with my life and work with Tara. My family had no

113

objections and I chose to use Govinda-Rose as my surname as well. Now we had a common name to support us. In one of our workshop days, during a meditation, I felt clear that it suited who I had become. I was growing rapidly, and needed a new name to support me in that.

Tara felt guided to write her first book *The Language of the Heart: is spoken all over the world*. She had been giving many lectures about how she came to her spiritual path, and it made sense to have it written down. Her life had so many challenges and awakenings. Her stories brought helpful teachings to people who were attracted to her as a teacher and healer.

During the writing of the book she developed constant headaches. When she asked why, in meditation, she was told how she had been tortured in a past life for speaking out, and the headaches were the only way to get her to push through her unconscious fears. She saw that she had been a writer in Italy, locked up in a room below the main street. Her jaw had been wired as part of her punishment for speaking out. In this life she was afraid of being tortured again. Tara pleaded with Spirit to be able to write the book in peace but the headaches continued. Tara rarely took pain-relieving drugs for any condition, but during the book she ended up taking extra-strong ones to cope. She was very relieved when the book was finally completed.

The Language of the Heart spoke of Tara being caught in wars, suffering abuse, and learning to deal with her own shadow nature. She also wrote of her near-death experience, and how she realised that heaven is actually here on Earth. The book became helpful in spreading the word about her work and spiritual life. Tara related how she had gone to India, visiting the ashrams of Sai Baba and Gurumayi, and eventually being told by Muktananda, in a meditation, to return to the West and be with her own teacher Ananda Tara Shan.

The book, for me, was a wonderful project. I was able to bring together many skills to help Tara create it. It was a joy creating something of value to bring into the world, and to further Tara's work.

Tara and I worked well together. I trusted her judgement with most things but stood my ground when it was important. We each carried painful memories of traumatic times, and when we triggered each other there was a deal of energy that had to be contained. Tara's high vibration and inner stress could trigger my anger, and I often had to cool my heels. I could also challenge her intensity at times but our love was strong, and it supported us through many demanding lessons.

It was Tara's nature to be driven, and often her fragile health got the better of her. My health was also a concern as I carried a fear of going beyond my means. My previous collapse cost me nine years of recovery and rebuild. Health practitioners, who had become good friends, were regularly trying to get us to slow down, but this was to no avail.

I often had to massage Tara's feet in the middle of the night, when she woke unable to breathe. We were fortunate that reflexology helped her so much, often preventing her from going into more life-threatening stages of the asthma. However, several times a year it did take hold and I had to take her to hospital. Many times the hospital staff had to give her injections as soon as we arrived. Hospital stays, overnight or for several days, became a regular part of our life together. The staff was very kind, often allowing me to sleep next to her bed to give what support I could. At least it kept us in the world, meeting and giving to people we otherwise wouldn't have come into contact with.

Sacrifice

Before I met Tara, I had been learning to fly single engine aircraft. I took one lesson per week and I had logged around twenty hours of flying time. I was just getting ready for my solo flight. Meeting Tara had delayed my lessons, as I had dedicated my time and income to supporting the work.

For some time now I had a nagging feeling that I was being asked to let the flying go. I tried to ignore this unwelcome feeling but it kept persisting. It felt like some higher consciousness was asking this of me, and I kept pleading my case. My main argument was that I could use flying to bring people to spirit. Like Richard Bach, through his inspiring books, I could help people know the divine within themselves through teaching them how to fly. But still the inner sense persisted, that becoming a pilot or flying instructor was not my right path.

Before we left for Denmark I booked one last lesson. To my great delight, that day I felt very clear in the head and flew the plane as if I were flying solo. It was an incredibly liberating experience. Suddenly I knew exactly what I was doing and the instructor allowed me free reign. When I returned from overseas, I would fly on my own and live my most heartfelt dream.

In Denmark I attended an Earth Healing Service. During the meditation I felt a radiant Light coursing through me, and it was very clear to me that it came from Jesus. I had seen him in visions before, but never felt him so close like this. The experience was ecstatic, uplifting and almost overpowering. I was being asked to give up studying aeronautics and study theosophy instead. I had never felt anything like this before and in the intensity of his Light I could only answer, 'Yes!'

It was an easy answer in an ecstatic moment but it became a mildly painful frustration for the next twelve months. I had said yes when in Jesus' radiance but then I had to suffer my personality withdrawal symptoms. It took time for me to let go of my absolute favourite activity in life. Giving up dance had been difficult enough but not flying was much more difficult. I had chosen my new course in life and I had to be careful that my frustration did not damage the benefits my choice was bringing. This was just another step on my spiritual path albeit, to my personality, a major one.

In Melbourne one day, Ananda ran a meditation asking the question: 'What does Love want of me?' My answer came, immediate and clear: 'Everything.'

I was content with this as it was straight from my heart. It seemed easier to give everything, rather than have to consider a specific task. The idea of 'everything' didn't hit any buttons at the time. Knowing that love is so important to this world, what could be more satisfying than to give my all? I had always been an idealist after all.

Again, what was felt in an uplifted state was more difficult to live in daily practice. I'm sure that one day it will become easier, as I learn to surrender my will to the Divine. It is regular practice that builds these qualities into one's character.

Learning to Serve

Tara guided me to become a better person, but sometimes in ways that I didn't appreciate. She would often come out of her healing room and announce that she had invited some friends for dinner that night. It was always a delight to have people visit so I was open to this. But then, just before she disappeared back into her workroom, she would let me know that she had clients for the rest of the day and I would have to prepare the meal. There was no request. Tara set me up for having to serve. It was good training but sometimes it pressed my grumpy button. Clearly, I hadn't reached enlightenment just yet!

06 - A Narrowing Path

By now my life was full of commitments. I was working days and nights as well as attending to many other things. One day, driving to the city in my old station-wagon, I had yet another other-worldly communication. This time, it came from the sun. It was a hot day and, in those days, I didn't have air conditioning. I had the side window wound down. I was taking a short-cut through the industrial area, when a stream of energy came down from the Sun, through the open window, and touched me in a significant way. Spirit was speaking directly to me from the Sun. I was being asked to sing as part of my service.

My first response was one of surprise. I could accept that the Sun was speaking to me but not that I was being asked to do more than I already was! I laughed in a way that expressed my exhaustion and questioned how could I possibly find the time? The next thing I knew, I was singing. Singing in the car, singing as I worked and doing various other things. I just started singing most of the time.

When Tara went overseas on a teaching tour, I used the time to learn a mantra song that used three simple guitar chords. By the time she returned I was feeling confident with my well-practiced tune. As usual, Tara immediately encouraged me to sing it in public and turn it into service. I was more than a little nervous but gave it all I had. It was the beginning of finding out that I could sing from my heart and that other people would enjoy my efforts.

This one song had taken me two months to master, but Tara immediately volunteered me to sing another song by the following Sunday. I took up the challenge and found a second tune. I was asked to sing in church, which felt like a very special duty. I knew that I could not allow myself any fear while I sang or people would hear it. I had to make a full commitment to share the song from my heart as well as play the right chords on my guitar. I had a tendency to close my eyes when I sang, as it helped me to connect with the full devotion in me, and to express my gratitude for consciousness. It wasn't long before singing became the most ecstatic aspect of my life.

Tara joined in by playing harmonium, and we both sang. Tara also asked others to play along with us, and we became part of many temporary bands. She also had us sing at every party we attended and even when visiting people for dinner. I have no idea how our friends went with all of this, but Tara was determined that we play and share the spirit of love and joy with all. Singing had meant a lot to her as a child, and continued to be something she loved to do. Tara also helped me to realise the potential in me, for manifesting the gifts of my soul in the world.

One of my favourite styles was gospel. It was all about getting into a groove and letting myself go. I felt like I was in a fire, becoming one of the flames and dancing about with the other musicians. I could sing with the qualities of one flame for a while, and then choose another. When inspired, I could change the dynamic of my voice, the meaning in the words, and how I felt at any given moment. It was very easy for me to open myself and just play within a song. If my ego tried to interfere, or any fears tried to take hold, I would just say to myself: 'I do this for God.' We only sang songs about the uplifting nature of love and sacred things, so it was natural that singing brought us many blessings. The music connected us directly with our souls and aspects of the Divine.

I began with guitar and then Tara joined in on harmonium. It wasn't long before we had added a large Native American drum and rain-stick, two Tibetan singing bowls, assorted bells and a didgeridoo. Tara had an interest in using sound for healing and we brought the music into our workshops for that purpose. Travelling interstate for work meant we now had an extra thirty kilograms in luggage. It was difficult enough travelling with our suitcases but now we had to consider many other logistics as well. Nothing ever seemed to bother Tara but I usually ended up as the one carrying things. That was simply more training. I can see that I needed a lot of it.

A Family

Tara got the idea to have Camilla, her dog, mated. Camie had eight pups and it was an incredible time watching her nurture and train them. One died, and Tara found good homes for the rest of them.

Camilla had always been an escape artist, being able to dig under any structure and run straight up the side of a two metre high fence. As she reared her pups, I was fascinated by the way she would encourage them to escape their enclosure. She would dig up an old bone and then walk around the perimeter, enticing each of them to make a break for it.

Tara sometimes allowed the pups to run free and Camilla would lead them off into the forest. Camie would return twenty minutes later, without them, and just sit looking towards the forest. Half an hour would pass and some of them would stagger back up the hill. An hour later again, some more would arrive. Camilla sat there in meditative stillness until each of her babes found their way home. I wondered if she was sending them a psychic message of her location to keep them connected to her. It was fascinating to watch how a hunting dog passed on her instincts to her young.

After each of them had found their new homes, one of the male dogs came back to us. He was bought as a show dog, but was too sensitive to handle the drugs that the owner was giving him. His name was *Sadhana* and he was magnificent. Tara and I got our exercise walking him and Camilla. Tara felt that it would be right to allow them to run wild for a time but we soon realised they would run for six or more hours before returning. He and Camilla would run down the side of cliffs, through the forests, and then not be seen again until after dark. It was inspiring to watch Sadhana cover many kilometres in just minutes. We ended up building a high fence to surround our house and the length of the property. Then they could run whenever they felt like it.

For nine years we were almost always travelling, mostly through taking our work on the road. We often toured in Scandinavia and went twice to the U.S.A. and New Zealand. We also travelled within Australia a few times each year, developing a school in spiritual healing studies. Another great blessing was participating in Peace Tours that included Israel, Egypt, Greece, Kauai, Australia, the U.S.A. and Canada. It was such a wonderful dharma to travel, teach, sing, and meet heart-centred people along the way. Denmark became like a second home to me, and Iceland also held a very special place in my heart. I became aware that in surrendering my desires to learn to fly, I had been given a travelling life in return. There were many blessings in sacrifice and surrender.

Our first trip to Scandinavia gave me a broader view of things. I now thought about and visualised the world as a whole. I had lived on each side of the planet and felt like a citizen of the world, awakened to wider work. On return from one journey, Ananda shared a Danish saying with us: 'When it rains on the bishop, it drips on the priest.' I took great delight in this as affirmation of the blessings I was receiving in just doing my best to keep up with Tara. It was always such full and satisfying work.

In the Shadows

Carl Jung wrote that there is 'no coming to consciousness without pain.' He suggested that we do 'not become enlightened by imagining figures of light, but by making the darkness conscious.' I found the spiritual path meant increasing contact with the Light of higher consciousness and getting closer to the Holy Grail of my soul. The closer I got to the higher Light, the more my shadow nature was revealed. Tara wrote: 'When I looked within, there I found the map for my journey ... I discovered anger, fear, guilt, grief, ambition, pride, jealousy, doubt, resentment, arrogance and depression. All of these I was not so keen on. But they were there in my shadow and I strove to bring them into the light, into my consciousness, so that I would come to know myself in truth.'

I acknowledged to myself that I had issues with anger and authority. I also had an idealistic bent, issues with money, and a craving to feel ecstasy in spirit. I wanted the world to be much more caring than it was, and I had to learn how to calm myself and find peace within regardless of outer conditions. I felt more empowered as I learnt to accept and welcome these shadow aspects of myself, bringing them into the Light.

Accepting that I had a shadow nature, mostly unconscious, was a major part of walking *The Path*. Aspects of myself needed to be acknowledged, accepted and integrated. The more I opened to the Light, the more my shadow nature presented itself. The more I accepted the truth of this hidden side of things, the more stored energy was released. In not trying to be someone else, I felt more peace but I had to keep working at it.

I had the expectation that spiritual life would be ecstatic but I was finding it to be a lot of hard work. There was karma to be neutralised and many feelings in my heart that needed healing. Most of these were from past-life traumas. The limitations of my earthly life were often frustrating. Perhaps in a previous life I had experienced the eternal and I expected life to be more like that. Instead, I was having to struggle through many challenges. I read Paramahansa Yogananda who recommended practicing being calm. I was not yet able to create this state enough of the time. I was still reactive and working through my programming and complexes. Spirit had given me so much grace but I still had to do the work of staying balanced and in the Light. I wondered, if in the end I might find what I sought simply by surrendering. I tried to do this by continuing my service, taking responsibility for my feelings, sacrificing some lower desires, and accepting suffering. There was joy in that, although it wasn't always easy. Some days I wanted to go within and never come out again. I knew that I had to learn to let go. I also had to accept and appreciate earthly life for what it was, while bringing Light into it. The key was to treasure the ordinary and learn to relax and trust more.

When I first began working on the anger within me, it was like learning to manage wild horses. My anger was intense and it was hard to hold onto the reins. I put in years of work in counselling and spiritual healing sessions, and gradually softened my defences. I also recognized a need to take training in martial arts, in order to re-program my response to conflict and as a way of acknowledging and containing the powerful forces within me. I learnt to channel the energy wisely. Whichever lives the energies were from, they were my responsibility now. I was learning that a true spiritual path is not for the faint-hearted.

Though Tara often pressured me in my development, she was also a brilliant partner in my healing work. She often quoted the phrase: 'You have to feel it to heal it.' While her energy sometimes brought out my anger, she demanded that I face it and repair any damage I created when it overwhelmed me. More than once I levelled the front door and reduced our dining room table to a flatpack. Tara would insist that I needed to rebuild any damaged items as my therapy. This taught me that I could not destroy without rebuilding. I wasn't angry often but, when it did surface, my anger was intense and destructive like a raging fire. The energies within me were being purified so I was more available for *The Cause*. The more work I did on myself, the more I awoke to the fact that I only wanted to be a force for love in this world.

Shifting Ground

A swami, visiting from India, ran a yoga retreat near our home. Our organisation provided accommodation for him, so Tara and I spent some time as his hosts. It was a wonderful week, helping him out and getting to attend activities at his ashram.

It became a week of uplift and joy. We got to speak with Niranjan (Swami Niranjanananda Saraswati) on many occasions, as well as attend his inspiring talks and workshops. He was a brilliant storyteller and brought a lot of joy and clarity to the yogic teachings. At the end of the week, Niranjan was offering people spiritual names. Tara and I lined up for this. Tara was given the name Tarajyoti and I was given Govindamurti. A 'jyoti' is an eternally burning flame; 'murti' means symbol, nurturer, and protector. Tarajyoti was certainly a flame of love and joy in the world and I was doing my best to protect and support her. On the final evening, Tarajyoti got up on the stage with her harmonium with a dear friend Kriyamurti, who sang. Swami Niranjan joined them on drums, and they played for us while 200 or more people danced and sang inside the marquee. It was an inspiring and joyful occasion.

The following week, Tara announced that she was changing her name again. She had sent off the legal forms to add 'jyoti' and make her surname *Govinda*. She felt that the '-Rose' had been amalgamated into the one name Govinda. Without speaking to me about it, she simply dropped the name we had shared for more than four years to establish her own. From now on, she would call herself Tarajyoti Govinda. This was quite confronting as I felt that I had been abandoned. I had a choice to make. If Tara kept moving ahead on her own path, I would need to get clear about my own.

We were flying interstate to run our healing school for the week. Unsure of my name, or even where I stood in relationship with Tarajyoti, I felt vulnerable and disconnected. I still had our old surname, which now meant nothing to me. It was a torturous week. I questioned myself constantly. For the whole weekend it was difficult being present with the students, as I was not yet able to be present with myself. Tara had thrown me in the deep end and it required me to take action.

On the Monday when our workshop was completed, we were taken to a local Buddhist retreat as guests. Over lunch, I spoke to our friends of my dilemma. It happened that we also spoke about swords. In a moment of quietude and stillness, I saw myself being handed a samurai sword on the inner levels. Then I saw the name that Swami Niranjan had given me, in the same shape as the sword. It was a precious moment, as I had always admired the beauty and form of the samurai sword. Here it was, together with my name, as a gift from spirit.

The following Sunday, in church, I received the impression that the name would give me extra strength if I ever required it. I also felt that it would bring some heavier energies that I would have to work through. Nothing too dark, but it was important to be aware that if I took this name there was material to be worked through. I chose to use it as my surname.

I had searched for my true name for much of my life but it had always eluded me. For over twenty years, I had tried many variations as I went through different stages in life. It was time to dedicate a healing to it.

The healer guided me towards relaxing and going within. She said prayers to invoke the healing energy and I went deep. The experience became intense. I felt my head under enormous pressure and I was frightened. I knew that I was re-experiencing something of the pain I had gone through at my birth due to the trauma of the forceps. I began seeing fearful images, as if my head was about to be crushed by a very dark force. I told the healer in case something was amiss, and she supported me in trusting and staying with this confronting experience. I did my best to stay conscious and allow the experience. When it finally ended, I lay quietly, allowing the healing Light do its work. Then I experienced a bolt of energy come down through the top of my crown chakra and out through the centre of my chest. At that moment a clear inner voice declared: 'My name is Arjuna.' The clarity of the information was extraordinary. This was a major opening in me. After a lifetime of searching, I finally knew my spirit name.

Work and study took up most of our time. I didn't see much of Tarajyoti for the next two years. She had been studying her Graduate Diploma in Psychological Counselling and stayed in the city most weeks. I would see her at home one or two nights a week, when she arrived exhausted and hungry. The dogs as good as took over the house while Tara was away; sprawling across the floor in front of the heater. Sadhana himself was taller than me when he was stretched out, so the two of them pretty much covered all the floor space between the front door and the bathroom. Tara would have to re-educate them each time she came back to the house.

Tara's studies were all-consuming. I became head chef and housekeeper and I worked with her on preparing her papers for the institute. Often we would work through until 5.00 a.m. and this was becoming quite wearing on me. I wasn't always happy in this work, but I carried on. After living this half-life for two years, when Tara finally qualified, we began work immediately on her next book. At the book launch of *The Healing Hands of Love: a guide to spiritual healing*, I wrote a poem to mark the occasion.

> *'Every day, less sleep,*
> *Every moment, closer to God.'*

It was meant to be humorous but it was honest as well. This was my experience of serving the cause of Love.

As well as Tara's studies, we were involved in many other things: establishing and running a Healing School; self-publishing and distributing her books; sacrificing paid work to overseas travel, and giving what time we could to voluntary work. Despite it costing us a fortune for her to study, Tara insisted on keeping her prices at a quarter of what she was allowed to charge as a qualified psychologist. Her focus was on keeping the services affordable to the people who were drawn to seek her help. It also meant that I continued to finance our activities with ever increasing loans from the bank. We mostly just covered the interest; the mortgage grew yearly.

Thankfully, the latest book *The Healing Hands of Love*, sold well wherever we travelled. It was our best seller. The Angels book also sold well but we had priced it close to cost as a gift to the angels who blessed our work.

The following year, with the support of dear friends, Tarajyoti and I worked through the winter to write, edit and publish her book *Becoming Whole: the psychology of light*. It was a major work, putting Tara's knowledge of psychology and healing into a complete text. It was another milestone to print and release it on her 40th birthday. We also put all of our spare time into developing a future teaching college, which would offer a two-year diploma course in Transformational Counselling. The book launch was also the birth of our new direction with this College.

The evening included our usual festivities: massive amounts of Danish cream cake and non-alcoholic champagne. No one got drunk, but we were all as high as kites on sugar and spiritual input. I sang with friends, and Tara and I both made speeches. Our launches were a wonderful way to let off some steam, especially after many months of truly gruelling workloads. The launches were always such special events, because they were a time to get together with co-workers and loved ones.

This particular evening felt extra special for me, as I was able to dedicate my work with the College to my beloved parents. My parents had supported me in getting my education, and it was through what they had given me that I was able to do this work in the world. I felt that I finally had something of significance to show for my efforts: the results of eighteen years research and personal investigation, as well as years running teaching courses with Tarajyoti. That night I felt most richly blessed.

Turning 40

Working with Tara, I was learning to serve. I was also learning about unconditional love, the joy of giving freely, commitment to cause, letting go, working through my shadow nature, and maintaining balance. Going on forty I felt that it was time for a reappraisal. I had been focused on the principles of *Love, Acceptance, Choice, and Will*, and these qualities were serving me well. But I felt an inner calling to step back a bit; to assess my health and balance. I was often stretched to my limit, and temporarily lost use of both hands from typing Tara's lectures into books, while making ad infinitum edits to them. I had been working extremely long and hard hours for many years.

Despite having work that gave meaning to my life, and often uplifting experiences, I was still searching to find satisfaction within myself. I had a need to let go of everything that no longer felt completely right. It was the blessing of turning 40 and it demanded I acknowledge it. I had to listen to my inner knowing that I had been pushing myself too hard for too long.

I met some resistance but I needed to slow down for a while. I had to be true to myself. Over several months, I made an effort to make less effort. I tried to identify how much rest I needed and which tasks I would no longer do. I wanted to work smarter, not harder. My signal that it was time to take a break was when I would dream of myself going out of control over a cliff!

Tarajyoti guided me to go within:

'Allow an image or feeling to come forth, that represents the wisest, kindest, most compassionate part of yourself.'

Relaxing, I went within. I entered a safe, sacred space. With the support of the healing energy, I saw an image of myself as a child, dressed in a white angora woollen jumper and standing in my grandparents' abundant garden. It was a sunny day and I was very young, surrounded by hundreds of flowers in bloom. Asking why I had difficulty trusting in happiness, I saw the image of a book cover showing industrial England; it was a book by George Orwell. I had, at some stage, developed a belief in hardship and mistrust.

I saw that when people challenge our 'inner child,' the child within us, the warrior or guardian sub-personality comes to the fore to protect this vulnerable part. I realised that when I came back to myself, to the love within, that this was where my strength and protection lay. In the support of the healing light, I could feel that I was protected when I loved. The answer was to drop the fears.

I had pushed myself to work harder but that had only increased the shell of fear that encased me. I had increased the barriers to love when I actually needed to open again and trust. The healing stimulated opening to a blossoming of love within. The healing light brought me to clarity again. I could see that if I renovated my house there would be room for me to dance. We did it. Much of the old house was gutted and a new space built. Now we had two-metre-high windows around us and a view of the beautiful Australian bush. It was a re-birth on many levels.

Spiritual Life

I continued to enjoy attending meditations and services for the Earth. In prayer I found sanctuary and purpose. It became clearer to me how humanity was in trouble, with so much suffering in the world. In meditating, I was getting to know myself better, and connecting with higher aspects of my inner being. In services, I became part of a collective voice, which prayed that humanity and the Earth receive help. In service I would call on the beings of higher consciousness to give humanity insight and awaken us, leading us to find our way to Love.

My studies in psychology showed me how, in being human, we have vast depths of unconscious life, as well as conscious choice. Theosophy was helping me to understand the many levels of consciousness that I am a part of. With so much of humanity caught in lower desires, I prayed that we might get through our individual and world crises.

Spiritual psychology was helping me to understand and be with my own nature, as well as to aspire to develop higher qualities. I was gradually awakening, moving from fear-based actions to wider and more selfless service. I was aspiring and working at developing character. To make my life of better service to love in this world.

In a way my path was becoming more narrow, but at the same time the options for contentment, were opening up. At least I knew where I was going, and I was graced by the very best company. Often in uplifted states; working with people of goodwill was indeed one of the greatest blessings anyone could be given.

The Spiritual Path brought many blessings and sometimes very specific ones. On one occasion, I had the following dream: I was kneeling, in the robes of a monk. Beside me was a woman, also dressed in maroon and yellow robes. I began to rise from the floor when I noticed the Dalai Lama, quite near, walking towards me. I bowed in reverence to his presence. He came closer, and I could feel the Lord Buddha behind him. I woke suddenly, feeling that a blessing of Light from the Buddha himself had been given.

07 - Fragile Times

*'Remember that you belong to no one and that
no one belongs to you. Reflect that some day you
will suddenly have to leave everything in this world –
so make the acquaintance of God now.'*

(Lahiri Mahasaya)

Some years had passed since renegotiating my working
relationship with Tara, and pressures had again increased.
Exhausted and experiencing an inner pressure, I retreated to
our bedroom to be alone and contemplate how I could go on. I
was seriously worn out. Unsure if I could continue to live and
work at the pace that we had been going, I needed a moment
to consider my future. This was a serious decision. In the space
of a few minutes, I was able to make the choice to continue. A
reassuring feeling came that, yes, I would be okay. I just needed
to feel that I had it within me.

My diary read: 'There is a time ahead for me, like a storm at
sea. I see it coming and try to ready myself for its impact. I've
known pain before and I have also known the growth that can
come from it. The child gets angry where the adult uses choice.
When I am able to remain conscious, I choose to do so.'

I asked myself: 'what outcomes do I want?' The answer in my
heart was that, I wished to create only peace and love. It was
early morning and I was asleep beside Tarajyoti. I woke suddenly,
feeling myself return from another place. The experience was as
if spirit had withdrawn from my body while I slept. I came back
into consciousness, aware that I had been out. I thought this
meant that I was soon to die, so I put all our paperwork in order
to make sure that Tara would be covered.

Tara became short of breath, trying to get relief using her nebuliser machine, but it didn't seem to be working this time. I massaged her feet, which normally helped to control the attack, but this time I had to call for help. The ambulance took her away, and drove forty minutes to the next major town. It looked like she would be in hospital for some time so I gathered her things before driving there myself. By the time I got to her, she was already in a hospital gown. It was a big shock to see her, as she reached out to me from the hospital trolley. Tara was covered in plastic hoses and medical drips, going in and coming out of her. She was looking directly at me with wide open eyes and an intense look of concern. I had never seen her look like this before.

There was frantic activity around her and many nurses in attendance. I was asked to sit in a small room until they had her stabilised. Before long a nurse appeared and shared with me that Tara was in a critical condition and that I might get a shock when I saw her. I had seen her in hospital so many times before, and I was ready to support her again. She was in Intensive Care, so I was fortunate to be allowed to be in there with her.

By the time I got to see Tara, she was in a bed but still gasping for air. She was now attached to even larger machines. I held her to give her all the energetic support that I could. Many nurses attended to her but it was some time before a doctor arrived who could give her the extra help she needed. Despite the best care that the hospital staff could manage, Tara still struggled to get her breath for something like fourteen hours. Her effort that day was beyond human.

When she was finally released from hospital, she had to surrender her time to resting. The most vigorous activity she was capable of was to walk very delicately around our local lake. Tara was uncharacteristically quiet. She could barely talk. She moved so slowly and everything about her felt delicate. Tara took to collecting pine-cones that had fallen along the pathway, holding them close to her body, cupped in the end of her T-shirt. I wasn't sure if they were for starting our fire at home or simply to collect things from nature. I believe it was more of a symbolic act than a practical one. Tara always loved life but at that time it seemed more precious than ever to her. She had already been through a death experience in 1984 and valued life highly ever since.

Tarajyoti wanted to keep working. I kept encouraging her to rest. She began to record meditations but I could see that she first needed to regain some strength. She was adamant that there were projects she wanted to complete but she just wasn't able to at the time.

It was a couple of weeks before Tarajyoti could leave the house. When she was able to go out alone, she wanted to see her friends. Though she was barely able to move or breathe, I knew it was something she needed to do, so I let her go. One evening she returned looking happy and at peace. She had recently had a misunderstanding with a close friend, and they had reunited. Tara had been to the Medicine Wheel near our church to share a peace pipe with her dear friend H-M. I couldn't believe that she had been out in the cold air while her lungs were in such a critical condition, but I knew this had been very important to her. Tara did her utmost to give love and support to others, even if it put her own health in danger.

We had been working non-stop for nearly ten years and her hospital visit had rocked us. We often gave each other spiritual healings, and I would facilitate Guided Imagery sessions when Tara had issues for which she wanted specific guidance. The sessions were conducted with the usual healing energies but the focus was on using active imagination.

Tara usually found it easy to get inner guidance, and this day she asked about matters concerning the College and her health. I would facilitate by asking her questions, and she would say her answers aloud so I could record her insights for future reference. This day the answer she received was very clear: 'You don't have to worry about anything. Something will happen soon that will be more beautiful than anything you can ever imagine.' Tara often received inner guidance to assure her not to worry so, in some ways, this was similar to usual. The main difference was the assurance that she should expect something 'more beautiful' than she could ever imagine.

Tara's health did not improve. We attended a four-day spiritual retreat that Easter and she had great difficulty with her breathing over the weekend. On Monday, it was even worse. She wouldn't go home and wanted to be present until the retreat concluded.

Tara had been quite reserved with me, and was catching up with many other people throughout the day. I felt that I should give her space, so I didn't have a lot of contact with her on that day. I had felt unusually withdrawn myself, not wanting to be in public more than I needed to. Something within me felt vulnerable and tender. It had started around the construction of the Medicine Wheel, and I hadn't been able to join in with making it. That was something I would normally enjoy being a part of, but ever since my dream of a storm that would bring much pain, there had been some inexplicable grief welling up in me.

Tara was hunched over, which showed the compacted state of her lungs. She sat quietly at afternoon tea time with a close friend Zachary. It felt somehow significant and I took a photograph of them. We then returned to the retreat for the last event of the day and I sat with her at the back of the hall. Ananda was speaking, giving the concluding talk. Soon we would all sing a final song and go our own ways.

Tara was still having difficulty with her breath but she refused to go home. I rubbed her back to help her to relax and breathe. I was quite concerned for her, but also knew that she would not budge from what she had chosen to do. I would just support her however I could. It was important to Tara to be there. When the day ended, Tara wanted me to help with the packing up and cleaning work, while she went off with a friend. A few minutes later, I was told that she had gone home. I left immediately to join her.

A friend had helped get her ventilator machine going, to help her to breathe. She was having more trouble than normal despite her prescription drugs. She had not been able to get the usual relief via the machine and was continuing to struggle. I called the ambulance but the service was reluctant to send help. I pleaded with them to come immediately, as I had given them all of the details they required, but the person at the end of the phone that day was uncharacteristically hesitant to order dispatch.

A close friend continued to help Tara get her breath, and another friend arrived who was an intensive care nurse. I left the house for half a minute to make sure that the ambulance didn't drive straight past. On my return I found Tara collapsed on the floor. I administered CPR but it didn't work. It was difficult to comprehend what was happening as I continued to try to revive her. The ambulance people finally arrived and took her straight to the local hospital, which was five minutes away.

I felt deeply sad for Tara, thinking she was about to go through yet another painful hospital process like the one she had endured only one month before. It would entail so many hours of suffering and struggling to get her breath back; such a huge and strenuous effort.

The ambulance left with Tara, and her two friends followed closely behind. I knew it could take hours until she got through the danger, so I collected some things for her hospital stay. I went to grab what she would need, but instead of the usual warm clothes and toiletries, I found myself collecting ceremonial items. On a practical level I had been doing everything possible to save her life, yet now I was in an altered space with an inner sense guiding me. It was as if I were preparing for a sacred ritual.

I collected her Native American moccasins, Inner Child cards and some other more spiritually oriented items that she might use when she came to. I had already placed a Native American blanket about her for warmth. There was a knowing within me that I was performing ceremony.

At the hospital there was a flurry. The doctors were exhausted from trying to revive her, and one of her friends was standing near her, singing a sacred song. The doctor looked to me with some concern in his eyes. He suggested that they had done all they could but I insisted that he keep going. He wanted to say something to me but my focus was only on getting Tara more help. Finally the doctor stopped. He had done what he could, and all that I had asked. The medical staff moved away and I sat there beside her.

I sat close and spoke quietly in her ear. I wanted her to know that she needed to become conscious again. I wanted her to know that I blessed whatever choice she would make but that her body would be of no use to her if she did not return soon.

I knelt next to her and touched her gently. My beloved was still. I told her that I loved her dearly, and that I was okay with whatever she needed to do. I blessed her, and let her go. I blessed her journey, not really believing that she might not return. I thought Tara had a lifetime of work to do here, and never thought she could be called away. I could feel that she was a million kilometres away and I didn't understand why. It was a very sacred time.

I spent all night in prayer, fully expecting Tara to return by morning. Then, I spent the next few years in shock.

Offerings

That week we prepared for her funeral. So many cherished friends came around and sat in our house. So many flowers had been sent that the entire place was filled. Tarajyoti had given so much love to so many people, and here it was, radiant in each of our hearts and in our home. We talked about times we had shared, and our disbelief. Many people phoned, and I felt like I was counselling everyone, helping each to deal with their grief. I could put some of my own grief aside at those times by being present for others.

Every single action I did, was like a ritual. Each moment held a sacredness and meaning. The world felt as if it had completely stopped, and everything happened in a kind of slow motion. It was a rare and altered state. Once, in a moment of solitude, I sat on the floor near the window, staring at the wall, immobilized by my grief. Camilla came over and sat beside me. It felt precious to be consoled by her. We had rarely managed to be close but now she placed her paw in the centre of my back, directly on my heart chakra. We were sharing the loss of someone we dearly cherished.

Ananda organised meditations and meetings, so that people who knew Tara could be given support in processing their grief. It was likely that it was also giving Tara the help she needed in passing over. Some friends held small services, and we gradually notified people who had known her. I made posters to let people know, and inviting them to attend her funeral. I attached these to trees and places around the town where we lived. The whole of Daylesford felt in an uplifted space that entire week. I was kept busy notifying people and making the funeral arrangements. Other friends took over the many aspects of making a beautiful send-off. For the whole week I felt like I was preparing a workshop, and that Tarajyoti would return on the weekend to help me run it.

Service

It was the morning of the funeral service and I was preparing myself. I knew that I needed to speak, and I was still working out what I might say. Everything else was just a matter of getting dressed to go. I choose to wear a special jacket that was a beautiful and colourful tapestry, hand made in indigenous style. It felt appropriate to wear something that was most special, and that also honoured the Native traditions that Tara and I had felt a shared connection to. It was time to come out of myself, and to be all that I could be, standing tall.

Two close friends came to support me, driving me to the church where the last rites would be held. When I went to the door, I enjoyed a huge laugh. John and Patanjali were both dressed in black suits and wearing dark sunglasses. They looked to me like the movie Men in Black, who had come to erase my memory.

In the car on the way to the funeral, I felt like a child sitting between my two brother protectors. I was very glad of their support. When we arrived at the Sanctuary I became aware that my grandmother was present in spirit, come to support me from the inner realms. Feeling her love, I nearly burst into tears, and prayed that I wouldn't until the service was done. I was touched by my grandmother's love that day. It was also very special that my family was there as well.

It was a grand service. So many people came to pay their respects to a life that had touched them. The church hall was filled, and I could see people all the way through to the bistro area. Tara had given so much love to so many people, and over so many years. She had boundless love and radiated joy on most occasions. Tara had always given without counting the cost.

I felt so uplifted on the day that I was concerned her family would think I didn't love her. I spoke with Tara's brother to assure him that my joy in no way diminished my love for her. Tara was very present in spirit and radiating her love through my heart. My joy was probably a mixture of her support as well as the shock, but I certainly felt in an uplifted state that day.

In the car with several friends, on return from the crematorium, one of them said she could hear Tara laughing. My friend could hear Tara saying that they should take me to the ice-cream shop. Tara knew that I enjoyed ice-cream and that I often ate some when I was feeling stressed. We were on our way to the reception but it felt okay to stop for half an hour. My friends' company felt so precious and it was nurturing to have that time with them. We sat around a table and talked about our favourite memories from childhood, when life had been simpler, and we so much more at ease. Another of Tara's friends felt that she could hear Tara reminding her: 'Don't forget the joy.' One of the most important lessons I learnt from Tarajyoti was to take every opportunity in life to be loving and to radiate joy. That was her keynote, I think. She had also taught that we should be responsible for all we create in this world.

08 - Healing Ground

In the week after the funeral, I felt I could go mad. I went to kill an insect but couldn't. In the heightened state I was in, all life felt sacred. For the first few nights, a friend slept on my couch. We didn't speak much, but just the sound of someone else in the house helped me to stay sane. Another friend recommended that I didn't stay in the house on my own but I didn't feel up to sleeping at anyone else's place at the time. The first night I tried to stay on my own, my mind nearly collapsed under the weight of darkness. I had to call someone immediately, and I slept in her healing room for a few nights. It was the only way. The following week I stayed at an accommodation place, in the lounge room on the carpeted floor. That helped me get through the first few weeks. I was in my sleeping-bag cocoon, alone but still around other people.

By day, my heart felt like it could burst, and my psyche reached for answers. My mind questioned Tara's guidance, that told her she would soon experience 'something so beautiful.' I wondered if she had known what that meant. I began to wonder about her vision of clocks when we first met, and if she had known that she had a short time to live. It would explain why she had worked so hard for so long. My mind was in a spiral. Hundreds of thoughts each clamoured for attention. Had I given enough? What if I could have given more? Why didn't I buy her more flowers?

There was an intense burning in my heart, of pain and loss and shock. Without Tara, almost nothing made sense anymore. Books on shelves that had previously felt so important to me now looked like dust. I found some relief in speaking into a Dictaphone. It made me feel like I had someone with me, hearing and sharing my distress. I never listened to those tapes but it helped enormously at the time. Another practice was in allowing my mind to go wherever it wanted to. I censored nothing, allowing my thoughts to go to any lengths in their enquiries. By not putting up any resistance, my mind simply wore itself out. It wanted answers but I didn't need them. I just needed to allow my mind to do its thing.

Another helpful practice was being very honest with myself. I got a large drawing pad and drew whatever came. They were random drawings, which became mandalas. I wrote long lists of my memories about Tara, including things that I loved about her as well as things that had challenged me. I represented positive feelings by open circles, while bothersome issues were dark and closed in. The size of the circles represented how much weight each issue carried. In this, I was able to allow and acknowledge my feelings and thoughts as they came to the fore. I could express and feel how happy or displeased I was about each element of our relationship. It felt therapeutic to put everything I could onto paper, and out of my mind. It was cathartic to be completely honest with myself.

Tara was gone, and at times I felt extremely alone. Sitting in hot baths gave me some relief. Forcing my body to relax quieted my thoughts. For several days I prayed in earnest that I could leave as well. My mind would search for any and every idea about why I had been left behind when my mission, I believed, was to be working alongside her. It helped to play Andrea Bocelli's album, Sogno, as loud as it would go. There was something in the way that Bocelli sang from the depths of his heart that allowed me to open mine, and allow the pain to flow. I also sang in church services but after awhile I needed to stop.

I was angry and hurt and confused. I couldn't comprehend why we had put all our resources into starting a college, if Tara would die before we even began. Lying on the ground, I surrendered to my grief. I tried to meditate, but I felt so cold. Seeking comfort, I curled up in the armchair by the northern window, to take some warmth from the Sun. Curled up in foetal position, fragile and still, I couldn't move and I had no wish to. I lay on the floor for days. Exhausted, I had become almost nothing. Close to not even existing. I surrendered to whatever it was that still held and protected me.

Tara's death triggered in me an attitude of 'Why bother?' I was convinced that anyone else I had anything to do with, in all likelihood, would probably also die soon. My mind, in its state of shock, expected everyone to die without warning. Nothing in life had meaning anymore. It became difficult to put any effort into my own well-being, as the thought also plagued me that I would also die. I saw no reason to make any effort anymore. I had given my all, but life wanted more. The grief sought to break me that I might become free.

Temporary respite came in the form of a dream. I met several loving women. The woman nearest to me offered to take me into the next world. She had radiant golden energy and I felt nurtured in her presence. I was relieved and ready to accept her kind offer to leave planet Earth. Then I saw some other people near me, practising Aikido. There was something about the activity that spoke to me as a symbol. I understood its message to mean that there was still work for me to do here. My choice was clear and I chose to stay. On waking I felt elated. This elation lasted for the next two days. I had chosen to stay alive and life felt very blessed indeed. But soon I felt the huge heaviness and burden of being in the world descend on me again.

I visited the Native Medicine Wheel at our church, and entered with respect. Standing there quietly, I felt a knowing that it was now my place to stand on the Earth. It was somehow important for it to be this way. For me to stay here without her I would get stronger, while Tara would go to serve where she was needed the most. The way the world was going, it needed all the help it could get, on the inner realms as well as here on Earth. I had received a great gift in meeting Tara and now I had enough experience and skills to carry on. However, this insight was no compensation for being alive. I still had to feel the pain, as we all do.

'The Lord giveth and the Lord taketh away,' challenged me as a very annoying truth.

Depression came and I had the idea to listen to what it might teach me. What I experienced, however, was that it would seize my spirit and take me into a void for several days. Each time I thought I could learn from it but each time it would just take me down and out.

Ananda helped me a lot during this time. She would often call me into her office and see how I was going with my work. Recovery would have been a near impossible task without her support. Ananda helped me identify my tasks and gave me some great advice: 'A knight acts' and, 'Never give up.' It was essential that I kept going. I have since seen a comparison of this with Winston Churchill's saying: 'If one is going through hell - then keep going!' The last place you want to get stuck in, after all, is hell.

I came across a Sufi saying that also gave me profound support. 'When the heart weeps for what it has lost, the soul rejoices for what it has found.' The idea came that gratitude was a key. One day, somewhere in the distant future I would be grateful, even for all the suffering and pain. I contemplated the day when I would be able to do this; when I would be able to understand the blessings in such a devastating loss. Even in the deepest of life's struggles – to be grateful for the journey, for the experience, for the very ability to be conscious. What an incredible thing we are a part of!

Despite occasional insights, I was still in the grip of intense and disorienting pain. I continued my search for ways to managing the grief and surrender to it. I decided to participate in a *Sun-Moon Dance*. Chief Joseph Rael (Beautiful Painted Arrow), who had travelled here from America, would run this three-day event not far from home. I knew almost nothing about it except that it involved being a dancer for three nights and days in a Native American style ceremony.

Initial preparation for the event began with a sweat lodge. A fire was in the centre of the tent and stones were added to the fire. The temperature inside the lodge was intense. It was only possible to breathe by restricting my breath as much as possible, or a burning sensation threatened to overpower my lungs. The sweat lodge was to purify us, before entering the ritual of the dance. Later that evening we gathered to enter the chamber, a large round structure, out in the open air. Various rituals were performed in the lead up to entering, and eventually we went in. Setting-up some simple bedding under a basic roof, I had my rest place for the next few days.

The musicians began playing and I entered the ceremony, dancing from the edge of the circle into the centre, and then out again. This continued into the night, and again throughout the next day. Usually dancing for twenty minutes and then resting for awhile. By the end of the day I was exhausted, not only physically but emotionally as well. I danced with mindfulness, aiming to manage the whole journey, and to maintain a pace that I thought I could carry for the duration.

After dancing for two days and nights without food or water, I saw a very brief vision of Tarajyoti while I was resting. She came to me as white light. I could see Tara's face clearly and was elated to see her. Her body was a stream of light, like a church vestment of white flowing cloth. She smiled at me and then withdrew. I desperately wanted to speak with her, but at least I knew that she was present and aware. Contact had been made.

By the second morning sunrise I felt empty and couldn't stand or walk without feeling ill. Supporters helped me out of the chamber for a time to bare myself to Mother Earth and surrender fully to what I was feeling. I cried and asked the Earth to take my pain, and that it help me to let go. I smelt the soil and gritted my teeth. I bowed my head and proclaimed that I surrendered my anger as well. I didn't know what the anger was, but knew that it was in me. When I screamed out 'Ho!' my carers knew I was complete. I was helped back to my feet and returned to my place in the ceremony. I cried as we walked, feeling my grief flow gently and easily, and then took some rest. Someone helped me to lie down, and a blanket was placed over me. One helper placed a wet cloth on my forehead and another over my eyes. I lay very still in a healing place. My carer told me that he loved me and, with my fists to my heart, I cried again in gratitude for the help. I felt the grief and let it go.

When the ceremony was nearly over, and the dancing done, the assistants gave me a small piece of watermelon. It was a three centimetre square block. Looking at the watermelon, I could see the veins of life within it. All my senses were heightened. When I finally tasted the fruit, I experienced a sense of belonging. I was part of One Life. The watermelon was so sweet and precious; it was a privilege to take in that life in order to sustain mine. Soon after, we were given a small glass with some water in it, and I had to just sit with it for at least five minutes. Slowly I introduced my body again to water, being very careful to not drink too quickly and trigger any rejection of it.

On leaving the ceremony arena we were guided to a large room where chefs had prepared one of the most magnificent feasts of food I have ever seen. After resting sufficiently, I ate mindfully and appreciatively, giving heartfelt thanks for the whole experience.

Withdrawing

Reading Yogananda brought the wisdom of sages to support me on my way. He wrote how the Divine gives us loved ones that we may learn to expand our love to others, but also allows death, so that we 'do not confine our love to only a few, but learn to give it to all.' I found it helpful to keep a broader view whilst also negotiating with the pain.

It is fair to say that I withdrew into my cave for some time, needing space to just be. I soon found that I was not able to function in the ways I had been able to before. It was obvious with music, as I could no longer keep the same timing as my fellow musicians, and eventually it became too painful, emotionally, to sing. In an impulse motivated by grief, I smashed my beautiful guitar, and fed the pieces to the fire. I was devastated that Tara was gone and sometimes angry at the challenges life was pushing on me. Despite my best efforts, the grief would plague my life for years to come, in subtle ways. I had done my best to serve love and open myself to it, and I had definitely found blessings in that. I had lived my life endeavoring to open to higher Love but now, without my beloved by my side, I felt exhausted and adrift.

Tara's death was really the end of my life, as well as its beginning. I can see, years later, how it was what I needed in order to find my own true strength, but it was also the end of my interest in being on the planet. It became difficult for me to find much reason for doing the work anymore. Life seemed to have constant disappointments. Tara had been my best friend, wife, partner, co-worker, healer, teacher, and muse. It was difficult to lose so much so unexpectedly. Life had pulled the rug out from under me yet again, and I would need some time to heal.

An Open Heart

I was so shocked by Tara's passing that I went looking to replace her. My heart was broken open and my mind in a searching place. I looked for my new partner everywhere, expecting that the Divine would provide. I felt a need for company and still hoped that I might have children some day. I sought refuge in nature, but winter was coming and the bare trees around the cold lake just reflected and intensified the devastation in my heart.

Tara and I had spent years establishing and promoting our teaching work. Everything had been put into it. We had run many talks and workshops during the years leading up to this, spending all of the money we had earned, as well as borrowing more. Tara had created a prospectus and I put six months work into promoting it. We established a college and had twenty-plus students enrolled for a two-year course. After all our work, Tarajyoti died after teaching for only one weekend and one tutorial. Now she was gone and I had to see the whole thing through.

Many of the students had felt close to Tara and were also in shock. The next year became an exercise in helping them to work through their grief, as well as train them to use the experience in becoming counsellors. One of the students decided to specialise in palliative care, and then many people close to her began to die. We were all being given intensive training, in very practical but challenging ways. Perhaps this was to be expected. Our work was esoteric, after all.

Tara had met with a psychologist on the day she died. I was hoping that this was significant, and that he might be able to take over as head teacher in the work. We got on well, but it soon became obvious that his way of working was different to the way I wanted the College to run. Trying to get this teacher on board felt like being in a wrestling match. I had to thank him for his help and look further afield for my teaching staff.

I attended many conferences in search of other Jungian-focused psychotherapists. I needed qualified practitioners interested in teaching and guiding my students through the next two years. Thankfully, I met several who were open to the idea. Psychologists, teachers, art therapists and even a Buddhist monk, came to share their expertise and caring hearts with my students. It was a difficult but fulfilling year, and the responsibility of the task helped to keep me above water.

When I had worked alongside Tara, I often felt the joy of serving a Great Cause. Without her in the physical world, the work was far more gruelling. Ananda became my rock, helping to keep me stable as I worked at doing my best. Ananda lovingly supported me with many meetings to manage this mountainous task.

Overall, the classes went well and I was happy with the quality of the education being offered but, within nine months, half of the students had withdrawn. Any money I could borrow was already spent on the College and, in my other work, I had consented to go without pay for the whole of the coming year. Things were difficult: I owed as much on the house as it was worth, and had to put it on the market. My only option remained to stay sane and just keep going.

As though she could sense these endings, Camilla had shown signs of wearing down for some time now, and I had been keeping close eye on her. One evening she seemed in pain, and I spent the night beside her, as she lay by the fire. This night it became obvious that she needed to leave the physical plane. I took her to the vet first thing the next morning, and she helped me to support Camilla to pass. I wrapped Camie's body in a blanket and took her to the car. Camilla had kept her distance from me for most of the time I had known her, but at that moment, I felt her full love. Camilla was in soul now and radiating such beautiful love. It was a very special moment as we said our final goodbyes.

I did my utmost to keep the College going, but in the second year most of the remaining students found other interests. The more options I created for them, the less happy they seemed to be. Each had their own preference for how they wanted the college to continue, and it was impossible to satisfy them all. After a year and a half most students had gone and, from a financial standpoint, I needed to stop offering classes.

Finding Love

Eighteen months had passed since Tara's ascension, and I hadn't felt much joy for a long time. I had the best support but I was lonely and began to demand of God that I meet my new partner. I was fed up waiting, and wanted some compensation for losing my co-worker and love of my life. My whining demands lasted less than a week. That Sunday morning as I was going into church, I saw a woman about to enter the room. Something about her, made it clear to me immediately that she would be my partner. My anger and demanding prayers now carried some embarrassment. I had behaved poorly. Feeling thankful as well as slightly apologetic, I wondered if I had been disrespectful in any way. In any case, the universe responded to my insistent prayers with love.

I wanted to get to know this person, and felt confident to speak with her that day. She radiated in a way that made her stand out from everyone else. Many who approached me wanted something from me, but this woman just seemed to give without expecting anything from me in return. Either that, or it was how I interpreted her disinterest in me!

Some days passed, and when I called her we chatted at length. This then happened a second time and encouraged my interest.

The day came to ask if it would be okay to get to know her better, but couldn't. I felt so much resistance and fear that I spent over half an hour summoning the energy to make the call. Once I did phone, I had crossed a line, and went to visit her.

In the beginning the relationship was quite one-sided, as all the interest came from me. I believed that spirit had organised our meeting, and I was hopeful that we might find love. I had a strong attraction for her, but I was also aware that I had been wounded by Tara's passing. I needed to care for myself as well as establish a new relationship. Most of me just wanted to surrender everything to love, but another part knew that I also needed to rebuild my own sense of self. There was much inner work still to do.

It may well be impossible to comprehend the true nature of any relationship, as there are always so many levels at play: two people's hopes and dreams, as well as fears and unconscious programs. I imagine that karma is involved in attraction, as well as the projection of one's awakening or ideal onto the other person. Opening to Gemma was certainly one of the most sublime times in my life. As much as we enjoyed the many gifts of our new friendship, we also had to work with our fears and inner programs as they arose.

I was filled with a bliss of having found my love, and annoyed many of my friends by announcing it regularly. I was overjoyed and couldn't help but share that around. In the face of any problems other people were having, I insensitively recommended that they just open their hearts to love. I was both out of my tree and on cloud nine. Others probably just saw me as being away with the fairies. I caught on to the idea of this when a friend I respected told me to go away and come back when I had settled down. It was not an easy message to take in when I was in such an altered and elated state.

Being with Gemma, I felt alive again. We enjoyed a lot of free time together, playing and going to the beach. There was a freedom to simply be, and this part of my life was wonderful and idyllic. Everything seemed to flow, with life smiling down upon me once again. My broken heart was filled with joy.

Gemma purchased a van, and we were able to sleep in it at the beach. During the day we would park the van on the ocean cliff and, opening the back lid, we had our own private room with a view. The area had a place where we could park away from the road, and just across from the water's edge. There was an amenities building and a hundred kilometres of open beach. In the middle of the night I could walk barefoot on the sand, and stand in wonder at the beauty and grandeur of the night sky. There were no fees to park on the beach, and it was as good as five-star quality. In fact, it was more like 5 million stars!

Life seemed perfect and our honeymoon extended month after month. I was very happy being with Gemma but eventually it was time to start coming back to earth. We shared about what we wanted in life and began to recognise some differences. One of my hopes with a partner was to finally have kids. Now for the third time in my life, children would not be an option. Angie had pushed them away, Tara would likely have died in childbirth, and now Gemma also had her reasons. That made three life partners who wouldn't have children with me. I guessed that it might not be aligned to my dharma in this life. I recognized that by entering the relationship before discussing any of our major personal hopes, I was giving away one of the main things I had hoped for.

The next twelve months brought mixed blessings. My financial fortunes changed and I was able to look to building a house. I put forward many design ideas and found that Gem and I had quite different ways of looking at it. We both wanted sanctuary, but I also wanted to create a community space. After several re-drawings of the plans, we settled for a home that included a studio for my public work. I also planned to re-create a peace garden that I had seen on Iona in Scotland.

While we were waiting for building approvals, Gem wanted to go to Vietnam and I was happy to support her in this. We went for a month there and experienced a fascinating culture. From Ho Chi Minh City through Hanoi, we met many openhearted and interesting people. The culture presented to us felt somewhat like an extended family, with many people happy to have us visit them. There were also some who expressed deep wounds, but these were only a few. The country had known so much pain in so many ways, and I wondered if this had been part of the reason its people had such open hearts.

Back home I got hands-on managing the house project, with a Krishna devotee as our builder. His spiritual dedication led to many interesting lunchtime discussions. In our initial meeting he gave me an inspired talk on Krishna Consciousness, and this opened me in ways I hadn't experienced before. His Krishna Consciousness was a powerful medicine.

The house took over six months in planning and a further six of hard labour to build. Most days I worked onsite from 7.00 a.m. through 8.00 p.m., and often later into the evenings as well. Sunshine, the builder, was a wonderful co-worker and also like a teacher to me. He pushed me to go beyond what I thought I could achieve. Either that, or he just wasn't aware of my limitations! I had spent the past ten years sitting at a computer desk. House-building gave my body a very serious workout.

As demanding as the task was, it was one of the best projects I ever took on in my life. It demanded everything from creative vision to very difficult negotiations with a council official. Contracts with tradespeople, attention to detail, thousands of decisions, and balancing economics were involved. It took all I had, mentally, emotionally and physically. My dear friend and mentor gave me excellent guidance, helping me to steer my way through any expectations of conflict, and stay focused on creating flow. This was incredibly helpful in such a large and complex project.

Occasionally building stopped for a day, and Gemma and I got to have some time together. We enjoyed cooking meals in our shed, or playing football on the land. Some Buddhist monks created a sand mandala in the local town hall, and when they dissolved it we were given some of the sand. We spread these sands on the land to bless it. Gemma also organised some earth acupuncture, which helped a lot in settling the energies after the building was complete. Gold mining had stripped the land bare in the 1850's and we did what we could to help heal the earth and support new life again. It took years bringing in fresh soil and animal manures, and then having to distribute it all. I busied myself planting shrubs and trees and invoking prayers so that the angelic forces might inspirit the place. The whole project was incredibly satisfying, and helped me to ground again. It was an enormous task, and such a great blessing to have the time and resources to create. It was such a beautiful thing, to develop one's own home and healing sanctuary.

Into Spirit

In November, without any warning, Ananda died. She had been very important to me for over twelve years and would be dearly missed. Her passing created some very deep processes, and many people I knew would take a decade to process the loss. Ananda had been my teacher, guide, beloved inspirer and support. Once again, my mind was spinning. I tried to take refuge in what Ananda had taught me over the years and to continue my spiritual practices.

When I reached out to share with others, I found there was no real avenue for that. Everyone had their own way of dealing with the change. I felt like I was on the outer. Supports I had depended on for all those years were no longer available. After several attempts at generating conversation and mutual support, I decided to go my own way for a while. I needed to focus on making a living, so I buried my head in my work. For over a decade my efforts had been dedicated to service, but now I had to be more practical and worldly. Thought needed to be given to what life required of me now.

I also identified a need to develop a paradigm that could support me psychologically during such unexpected changes. I wanted a foundation that gave meaning to life, and dedicated time to study and to intuit what was essential to my life's path. After much consideration, I came up with a five step plan that encompassed all I felt was needed. My main foci would be to: *Relax; Trust; Serve; Appreciate; and Merge with the Divine.* If I could find trust in life, and appreciate that there was value in all experiences, then I would be open to life. The more I could trust, surrender and let go, the more likely I was to be able to be at peace with Creation and enjoy its blessings. The way to receive insights would be through relaxing and meditation, and in selfless service I would begin to merge with That which creates, sustains, and serves all

When I looked for Ananda on the inner levels, I heard her say: 'Look to Maitreya' (to the Christ). I had always looked to Ananda as my teacher, but now I was being directed to look to teacher's Teacher, to the guru's guru. Ananda had given her utmost to awaken me and many others to the Light, and it was here that I now needed to focus. In a healing, I saw a vision of a large rock in a river. I could feel that Ananda was asking me: 'Which is stronger, the rock or the river?' It was obvious which I needed to be. I needed to flow.

Overdrive

In the introduction to Richard Bach's book *Illusions*, I found one of the best encouragements for living life that I had ever come across. In Bach's short story, he wrote that: 'The river delights to lift us free, if only we dare to let go.' My aim was to go with life's challenges, but I also had to search within. I was still trying to deal with my grief for Tara, and now for Ananda as well. Increasing pressures weighed on my shoulders and my shadow nature came more to the fore. I was also concerned that I might lose my way, and so I increased my efforts and dedication to the work. However, the thing I most needed to do was relax. Tara's death had left me confused and fragile, and one of my ways of dealing with it was to try to continue what I had done before. Sometimes I went bull-at-a-gate, striving to make time for that work, as well as to fulfill my many other tasks. A part of me was driven to charge into battle for the Cause, but I was unable to relax enough to know what that even meant anymore. I often felt mild panic around not serving well enough.

My inability to relax also complicated my relationship with Gemma. It meant that I withdrew myself in some way. In not dealing well with the stress, I was less available to my partner. When I did reach out to her, I found that she was often in a place that I just couldn't get to. Perhaps our individual natures were connected to very different stars, even though we shared many positive aspects. I made the mistake of repressing my grief, thinking it would make the way easier for Gem. Of course I learned that this doesn't work, but at the time I was trying everything. I did all I could to give to Gemma, but for a short time I became impatient and frustrated. It became difficult for me to find closeness. Gem felt things so deeply, and I was used to just pushing ahead with projects. It took a lot of effort for me to be able to switch from my default setting, and be more available, in my feelings. I thought that my heart was in the right place, but now I had to learn more about opening to just being present and loving.

Bhakti

For several reasons I hadn't sung in years, but it was still something that sat deep in my heart. When our dear friend David returned from Canada, he invited Gemma and I to sing with him in a new band. It was such a fantastic opportunity. We teamed up with another dear friend Greg. We called ourselves *Bhakti*, meaning devotion, and gave concerts on each full moon. Our music focused mostly on the sacred, and the songs ranged from 5,000 years old to those that were written just last week. David provided many beautiful songs and Gemma and I added to that. We mostly played mantric-style songs in Sanskrit and Tibetan, as well as some English and Native American ones. It was incredibly satisfying to be able to express myself again in this way.

Gemma and David made promotional posters worthy of an art gallery, and I distributed them around the local towns. Gem played with sensitivity and beauty, while Greg's keyboards complimented perfectly. David and I often found a groove in which we could improvise in our singing, losing ourselves in the energies our prayers had invoked.

Singing was an ecstatic experience for me. It was the time when I could feel my higher nature activated. When I sang in church, I often experienced profound energies. One day, I felt the space above my crown open up at many levels, and then vibrational energies descending from those heights. In concerts I felt like a generator, where prayers came to me during the songs. Like the conductor of an inner orchestra, I directed blessings to where they were most needed in the world. The music opened me to my soul nature, where I felt aligned to sacred work. In music, I was as alive as it was possible to be.

With the house nearly finished, Gemma came up with the idea of running a community-based Laugh Club. She had seen it on the TV and asked for my help in establishing one. The idea of laughing with a group of strangers each week did not initially appeal to me at all. I was still in multiple levels of grief and I would rather the idea had gone away. Gem was keen though and had organised to try it out. Being reluctant to miss out on an adventure, I went along with her for the day. It was a half-hour session and felt very welcoming, playful, and a lot of fun. It was very much like having the freedom of being a child again. By the end of it I felt so charged with positive energy, I wore a smile on my face for the rest of the day. I made the decision to support Gemma with her Laugh Club, and attend for a few sessions to help her get it underway. Those three weekly sessions became a four-year project for me.

After getting a handle on it we also developed it into a business, promoting to organisations and corporate clients. We gave the free sessions every Saturday, and during the week I took the work out to the wider world. Donning a fancy suit, I presented myself as a consultant on stress management and guided people in having a laugh. For a while it was my quest to help people find release from stress, and share some understanding with them of holistic psychology. I hoped to help others to connect with the joy of life by giving them some tools to manage difficult times. I worked with corporations, government workers, prison guards, retail managers, mentally handicapped people, rape counsellors, drunken accountants, and school teachers -- amongst others. Every client group had an entirely different psyche, and it fascinated me how I could make it work for each of them.

It was an intense practice being sensitive to people's different levels of fears and unconscious material, and guiding them through their processes into open and playful fun. I was privy to see just how much tension some people carried, and how much joy they experienced when they let go. I thoroughly enjoyed the task for a couple of years, but in the end it became too stressful for me. Organisations would usually insist that their workers take part and because of this I often met with antagonistic attitudes. Also, it was a new health practice, which took many years of work in research and promotion, so it was producing too little income for us. The mortgage was getting larger, so I looked for a job.

In my consultancy work I had generally only entered organisations for one to three hours at a time. I began to wonder what I could give to organisational and staff well-being if I became part of the organism itself. A new challenge presented, and my inquisitiveness was perked.

Forty minutes drive from where we lived, was a small city where a large organisation was looking for staff. I had no real idea what the job entailed but I could see that I could work creatively with others, as well as enjoy a regular pay. My tasks included interacting with an international public, and I enjoyed this aspect very much. It was the perfect job for me in many ways, as each day I got to role-play with the visitors. The job included entertaining as well as informing, and I got to enjoy using my acting skills. Every day people would take my photo, and I delighted in the idea that my smile was travelling with them, to cheer whomever viewed those images in the future. I loved world travel, but here the world travelled to me. Whatever light I could radiate, would now go back out around the world in the photos, and in the hearts of the people I met. My love of life and people now had a vehicle for expression. The initial joy lasted at least a year, and then I just set my intention each day to maintain it. I was enthusiastic about the work and how each day would unfold anew.

At work, I became aware of some disgruntlement in people. There were the usual negativities and general carry-on, but it seemed to worsen with management putting much of their attention to the Global Financial Crisis. More than once we were told that it was our wages that were the problem, which, I believe, began to undermine staff connection and confidence. Management put their focus on increasing attendance and sales, while I thought that we needed to keep our attention on customer experience and staff welfare.

Meetings seemed to become more serious, pushing specific agendas. New training sessions were all focused on sales. We were moving from being a service-based organization to stressing about retail. It may well have just been within myself, but I thought I noticed an increase in staff frustration, and a sense that we were not valued by the organization. It seemed that joy was being dismissed and devalued, and I wondered how much fear was becoming the driving force. I continued to request communication with upper management to share some ideas but was brushed off on several occasions. I was only a member of staff but wanted to give what I could and, ideally, to build bridges between staff and management, in order that we might all actualise our potentials.

Some of the ways things were done started to get me down, but I also continued to enjoy many of my roles. Any hour of any day could bring completely unexpected joys. Regardless of having vastly different interests in life, I had great affection for the people I worked with, and the aspect of play within the job was sometimes sublime. They were a wonderful group of creative people, and it was a joy to work with most of them.

Yin and Yang

Gemma and I were complimentary, but also quite different in many ways. One of the aspects I most enjoyed in life was the times we got to relax together. Gem was a very sensitive soul from whom I was learning a lot. Like me she liked quietude, and she kept to herself a fair bit. We both enjoyed sanctuary from the world, but the idealist ideas-driven aspect in me needed to constantly create, and this might have been a bit much for my dear companion at times.

I continued to struggle with finding balance, giving what I could to the relationship, work, and family; also, meeting financial commitments, and offering wider service to the world. I felt a need to study, and at least work towards creating something that I could offer humanity at large, even if I was not in a position to offer much at that time. I was never sure if I was being driven by my soul's purpose, or simply by my grief. All I really knew for sure was that I had to continue working for love in the world. I also needed to garden to help ground myself, and I enjoyed creating beauty. I seemed to be working most of the time, as well as struggling to pay the bills.

The very best days were when I surrendered, and just went with Gemma to the beach. It was an hour and a half drive from where we lived, but at the ocean my mind would let go and I would find clarity and peace again. I also got inspiration there, and solved many things that had been on my mind for weeks. Gemma knew what was good for me. We would walk for hours, or sit in a café or beneath a tree. Life felt worth living at these times.

In my spare time I read a lot of spiritual texts, including those by Paramahansa Yogananda. Yogananda wrote about seeking the Divine as one's first task in life; to 'meditate earnestly' if one were to find God. With so many things challenging me in outer life, I looked more within. I continued having many hot baths, seeking to subdue the physical and allow my mind to disengage from stress. I needed to connect with spirit, so I meditated whenever I could. I began connecting with a sense of peace, and occasionally felt some bliss. I often felt uplifted when singing or listening to music. I was seriously looking for the Divine as Yogananda had recommended, and I was feeling some positive shifts.

One day, while driving to work, my attention was drawn upwards. An energetic presence came through the entire breadth of the open sky. It was the largest energy I had ever seen in my life. For an instant, this giant consciousness presented to me like it was saying hello. I cannot claim that it was God as such, but I do know that it was clearly an aspect of That. It was well beyond human, and of a different realm to the physical.

Rumi wrote of moving towards the Divine, as a step 'towards the Lion.' He speaks of it as a 'great and rare matter,' the 'true step in a human life,' and says that, in contrast, 'the rest are mere footprints.' Outer life was interesting enough, but inner life was calling to me more.

Pulling Up Roots

Gemma kept wanting to move, and I didn't see any point in staying in the house if she wasn't happy. I put many of my days off from work into completing the garden, as I wouldn't be free to sell until I had finished the project. In between other commitments, I spent most of my spare time working the land. I would have preferred to stay put but I made the choice to stay with my beloved. I was already strained trying to make sense of life. In working towards putting the house on the market I felt a loss of my roots. Daylesford had been my home for more than twenty years and I was a little uneasy with the thought of leaving there. It was also my spiritual home, as was soon to be emphasised.

Probably as a distraction, I considered making a journey to India to visit the holy mountain *Arunachalya*, once home to the revered spiritual teacher, Sri Ramana Maharshi. Almost immediately, a voice within me made it clear: 'This is your Arunachalya!' I was being told that the land beneath my feet was my holy mountain, and yet there I was preparing to leave. This concerned me and I would need to meditate on it. I continued to work on finishing the house and spent a couple of years getting it ready to put on the market. The time was coming closer when I would have to consider saying my goodbyes. I acknowledged to myself the efforts I had made in building it, and the importance of not attaching to the results. I recalled that during the building work, Sunshine the builder had often impressed upon me that our task was to make positive endeavor, and whatever else became of the work was not our concern.

The idea of letting it go brought some sense of loss but not as much as I thought there would be. I had put so many efforts into creating this house and home over the past eight years, but I was soon to leave it behind. I took some refuge in the idea: 'Not by what I have, but in what I am able to live without.' I called on the help of angels to support me with the shift when three kookaburras arrived and sat on the TV aerial in front of me. They chuckled: 'Ha ha ha.' ... 'Ask and ye shall receive.'

An End of Dreams

When she was alive, Tara would often appear in my dreams. I took this to mean that she represented the inner feminine aspect of my psyche. Now, without notice, I was still dogged by dreams of Tara dying or dead. Perhaps once a month, I dreamt of her telling me that she was going to leave the relationship. I assumed this meant that at some level I hadn't let go of her yet, but I was never really sure. It was nine years since she had passed but still the dreams presented. I imagined this as my psyche still adjusting, my inner and outer realms not yet fully aligned. I watched as life stripped me bare of more attachments. And perhaps I just wasn't standing my ground.

Increasingly feeling displaced, on my birthday I asked myself: 'What can I do that will express, more deeply, my soul and spirit in matter?' I wanted to know: 'Just what is my masterpiece?' and, 'What do I need to create in this life, to be fulfilled?' There was a longing in me, and a need, to give this world my absolute best. I often contemplated the inevitability of my death, and I had a desire to leave a legacy. Even if it was only that I could say as I left: 'I have loved.'

Loosening some of my connections to house and home, I looked to God and to going home into Spirit. I began thinking about my next incarnation to help me to cope with this one. I was being stretched in many directions: what my wife wanted; what my work wanted; what my personality wanted; and what my soul called for. In the middle of life's general busy-ness, I just tried to do my best.

In August, I dreamed of Tara telling me that I didn't look 'well, happy or energised.' I told her that I felt that she had left me. Tara offered me dates and raisins, and I tasted how sweet they were.

Time Away

There was quite a deal of stress around getting ready to sell and move. I thought that Gemma and I needed a break and we headed to Nepal for the month. Our journey there was to be challenging as well as fascinating. I felt blissful excitement seeing Kathmandu again from the air, but definite culture shock on landing. I had always remembered Nepal with positive regard, but on this trip it would take most of the month to acclimatise. I felt intense stress in Kathmandu but still found the heavenly bliss close by, in simple village life.

We located a Buddhist guesthouse five minutes walk from the Stupa at Boudenath, and made it our base. Every day an entire community would visit, and walk in clockwise circles around the giant structure there. Thousands of people were chanting 'Om Mani Padme Hum'; we joined in at least twice every day. It was special to be part of an entire community at prayer. At the end of half an hour of chanting and moving meditation, we would climb four or five flights of stairs, and sit on a café rooftop overlooking the area. The beauty of the Stupa at Boudenath was such an inspiring sight.

On a day when Gemma wasn't well enough to travel, I ventured out with a tour guide. He was the son of Tibetan refugees and helped me gain access to monasteries in the local hills. Our taxi managed to get half way up the mountain and we had to walk the rest. With special permission I was allowed to sit in prayer with the Tibetan monks. As they beat their drums, chanted, and blew on huge horns, I also prayed. Understanding my interest in spiritual life, the guide organised entire days for us to visit temples of many different religions in the Kathmandu valley. On one of the journeys back into town I saw a sign painted on the back of a truck. It read: 'By Love is Life.' To me, this was the underlying spirit I connected with in Nepal.

Our stay became increasingly stressful as it was at a time of heightened political strife. Most weeks brought day-long strikes.

Taxis were being stoned and sometimes set on fire if they drove on those days. It became tiring to have to hide ourselves in the back of taxis, so as to avoid igniting any trouble. After a few weeks it began to feel too dangerous to travel around some places, and there was no telling how far the agitation would go. There was some official vote to be made on the weekend and we changed our flights to avoid flying out on that day.

On our last evening there was a special ceremony at the stupa, and every person in the entire surrounds participated in some way. Even the rubbish truck decided to do its rounds in the middle of this huge event. There were thousands of people, general noise, monks chanting, people talking, exotic smells, constant movement, brilliant colours, and electric lights. The stupa was lit up and the alleyways were filled with lit candles, in use as prayer. It was exquisite. My senses opened to take it all in. As the evening developed, I became at one with all that was happening there. I opened to the prayers of this magnificent occasion. For me, that one night was worth the entire journey. I was completely engaged in the wonder that is Nepal.

We had already used up our holiday time, but I was aware that we were both now quite stressed from the past month. I somehow managed to convince work to let us have some more time off and back in Australia we soon headed North. In the warmer climes of Stradbroke Island, Queensland, Gemma and I settled in for a needed rest. There was almost nothing to do there except relax, read, and walk along the ocean cliffs. It was inspiring just being in the peaceful nature and watching whales passing by.

I took a book with me that I had considered reading for many years. The book titled *When Daylight Comes* was about the life of Helena Petrovna Blavatsky and the activities of the Theosophical movement in the late 1800's. Reading the book, I felt a connection to this past time. I had already received an impression twenty-two years earlier that I had been around Blavatsky in that life, and now, as I read, I could feel a subtle alliance with it. In some ways, this was perhaps the beginning of my knowing, that I would someday need to return to my Theosophical connections. Theosophy speaks to world service and I knew within me that this was my true place in life. This was the calling that I had wondered about. I could only hope that Gemma would want to be there with me, but for some time now, I could feel her steering towards other interests.

Back home in Daylesford, still in the house, I was sitting on my bed contemplating something I had read. The author was suggesting that human thought is on the edge of the Divine's greater consciousness, and that our desires, hopes and dreams, cause the Divine to expand. I was not sure about the truth of this, but thought it interesting enough to explore in a meditation.

I relaxed my body and my mind, and I focused briefly on my breath. I put my attention on my face, and imagined for a moment that it was indeed, at the edge of All That Is. The next five minutes or so were the most profound I have ever experienced in my life. I found myself aware of a vast space within me. This space, within my own conscious being, actually went for forever. I experienced infinity within me, and I felt how it went in every direction I put my attention. I was being allowed to 'see' all that was within; that 'All' is within.

As my consciousness returned to my mundane existence, I put my attention back onto my body and the outside realm. After experiencing this grace, I wondered why I had been given such a blessing -- such incredible access to such a profound truth.

Around one week later a black bird flew into our fence and I had another glimpse of the infinite. Gemma went to its aid while I restrained our cat and dog. I looked at the bird and it seemed to be dying. Gemma was supporting it, and what struck me was the look in its eyes. It was looking at me with very clear intent. When I accepted its gaze, I saw in this bird's eyes a window to the eternal universe. The same world that I had recently seen within my own being, I now saw here. The bird, as such, was now a vehicle for me to see Divine Love. The Infinite space was showing itself to me, through the eyes of this dying bird. I was aware of the whole outer scene, but these eyes were a window to God's Love. I can honestly say that it was the love of the universe showing itself to me. An infinite, eternal Presence of Love.

Many experiences were there to help me find my sense of direction. One day, listening to the sound of water trickling across rocks in the forest. I felt the delicate nature there. There were Angels, perhaps, or nature spirits. I took the moment to feel and appreciate a precious sense of place. I needed that in my life at that time.

Back at work again, I asked myself the question: 'What would I like to be doing in life?' The answer came as another question, together with an answer ... 'What do I feel like doing right now? The future can wait!'

Choices

The house sold, that October I said goodbye to the town that had been my home for twenty-two years. I felt like a seed blowing in the wind, wondering where I would land when all these changes settled. We gave a thirty-day turnaround to the buyers, but then found that there was nothing for us to rent. With one day to move, we finally found a rental property that allowed us to keep our pets. The house was near to a city suburban creek, and only a four-minute drive to work. On the face of it, we had settled.

Adjusting to being in a city, after living near nature for most of my life, was quite strange. I also had to adjust to not having a garden or forest to walk in. Gemma was much more into the lifestyle there, and we would often eat out. It had its benefits, but it was also very foreign to me. City life felt quite bleak compared to where we had come from. I made the most of living there and joined the gym. We also walked in what nature there was along the suburban creek. I kept applying myself to my work and writing articles on books that inspired me. I was managing, but there was something not sitting right in my heart.

When I was home alone, it became obvious that the house had only small windows, and I had no contact with nature when inside. The house and town started to feel like a temporary abode for me, and I struggled to find peace. Gem's focus went to her work and making many new friends, and my focus was on study and building an online educational resource centre. I also continued editing and publishing Tarajyoti's writings, so people had access to her work. That December, after only two months in the new house, I dreamt that Gemma wanted to leave me. Within the dream, I asked her to please do it over time, so I didn't go into shock. It occurred to me, that I may have well have been put on notice.

Dismissed

Pressures at work continued to mount, quite possibly linked to feeling disheartened at home. Work had changed its focus, and I was still arguing philosophical differences with some of the near to upper management. My creativity often felt stifled, and I was frustrated in being unable to contribute more to the place. I was also concerned for staff welfare and wanting to have more input into developing the culture there. I wondered whether my soul wanted me somewhere else, or just to learn from the limitations. In the midst of this I had a dream where I was atop a great wave, and about to be dropped from this lofty height ... I relaxed, trusting that I would be okay, but aware now that something was soon likely to change.

An incident occurred at work. I felt very disappointed and considered calling in the union. I wanted to avoid creating conflict and instead argued my case with one manager for a whole week. I pleaded for understanding but felt like I was just being stonewalled. I knew that I couldn't accept the conditions she was placing on me, and that some major shift was about to occur, though I had no idea what it was going to be. One morning, while setting up for the day, I put on some music. The song that came on was Bob Dylan's 'Song for Woody' (Guthrie), a very relaxing song. As I listened, I felt that too many things had been wearing me down. Dylan's lyrics reflected how I felt, planting the thought, '... leaving tomorrow, but I could leave today. Somewhere down the road, someday ... ' The music spoke to an aspect of me that I was near to not caring like I had before. I gave all that I could to my workplace but was becoming increasingly disillusioned. I had to acknowledge that, in not making any headway, I was getting fed up. With one issue, even the simplest of changes had taken me over two years to negotiate.

Looking back, I still have to question myself about how much the environment I was in simply reflected conflicts within my own being. It is too easy to blame others or circumstances for our own learning. The conditions certainly became more frustrating, but they were probably exactly what I needed for the unfoldment of my soul's purpose and the developing of my character. The workplace and relationships with others were the very stuff of my learning and growth. I was impressed by Carl Jung's insight: 'When an inner situation is not made conscious, it appears outside as fate.'

Separation

Sitting on the couch one evening, Gemma shared that she wanted to leave. I had contemplated this happening some day but it still took me by surprise. I sometimes wondered what would happen as I got older and our age difference became more significant, but I also felt very deep love for her and was committed to the relationship. I had only recently written in my diary how I felt Gemma to be 'loving, kind, and considerate,' and that I felt 'uplifted, nurtured, loved, befriended, and supported in her company.' When I heard Gem share where she was at, I remained seated to let it sink in.

There had been many pressures for some time now, so to some extent it made sense. It wasn't my preference but I had to accept it. The past year felt like I had been making too many compromises that I was not at peace with. I had given all I could so, at that level, I felt okay. My choice was to love and be loving however that needed to manifest itself. The important thing would be to avoid believing that I was a victim in any way.

Part of me was happy for Gemma, that she knew what she wanted in life and had the courage to pursue it. Another part of me was quite confused. At the time it was beyond me to understand why things were changing so drastically. Was my soul, or each of our souls, orchestrating this? My guess was that we had both given the best we were able and, because of our individual growth, we were now ready to walk our own paths. As usual, I cut off from my feelings about it so that I could take action and deal with emotions at a later time.

I wasn't sure what to do, except to think things through. It had taken me nearly nine months to move all of our things from Daylesford across to the rental house, and now I had to move everything again. I sought professional help, and the psychologist helped me to face various fears around how I might cope. He also helped me to look to what I needed to do for my ongoing well-being. I questioned what I could do to distract myself when the grief would emerge. I knew that I would not feel it for some time but it would eventually hit. That is how it had always worked with me.

I also knew that it would take me time to find my balance after we parted, and I requested some leave from work. I didn't want to go to my job and find myself in tears. My immediate management was very understanding and kind enough to grant me six months off.

I wrote poetry to help me connect with my feelings.

> ' ... I do what I can
> to tread the way,
> to become the kindness,
> that counts not the cost.

So I fill these years,
in my practice, seeking peace;
And learn to befriend,
this heart of mine.'

(A. Govinda)

Starting again

I smiled at finding Henry Longfellow's idea that 'the best thing to do when it's raining, is to let it rain.' I had no real idea of what I was going to do except leave. Travelling light seemed the best way at the time. I let go all of my household goods yet again, most of it brand new. Anything Gemma didn't want, I gave to a charity organisation. I kept one work desk and a comfy office chair, which I imagined would be enough for my next stage of life. It was a return to the realm of Zen, in the hope that I might find peace in simplicity.

Our parting was mostly congenial, and I was very grateful for that; to be able to approach an ending without creating unnecessary dramas was important to me. Like something in the twilight hours, the separation didn't cause me immediate emotion. However, I spent the next two years trying to process what had happened. Parting with Gemma left me confused for a long time, and I was essentially in mild shock, trying to understand what happened.

After saying goodbye, I got in my car and headed North. Free of the city, I removed my shoes to feel something of the freedom of being on the road again. Barefoot and fancy free. I was doing my best to accept that life, yet again, was sending me on my way. I was both happy for Gemma, and sad and confused for myself.

I had loved her dearly but, yet again, I was alone. For the next two years I would fluctuate between grief, confusion, anger and contentment. Bob Dylan's lyrics were still playing in my head: '... he not busy being born, is busy dying.' I went on my way and made the most of my circumstances.

The poet Basho wrote: 'When the house burns down, you own a better view of the rising moon.' My life was again a bare canvas, but I had survived change before. Previous invitations from life to stretch myself had given me many gifts, and developed inner strengths. Despite feeling homeless and somewhat abandoned, I knew I needed a focus. I had been reading about distraction as therapy and this would be one of my practices.

A year later, I met with two psychologists who insisted that I needed bereavement counselling. They were of the opinion that I hadn't completed my grieving of Tarajyoti, and this had sabotaged my ability to open up to Gemma. Considering the amount of pain I had gone through after Tara died, I had a lot of difficulty in accepting this, but surrendered to their help.

09 - The Road Forward

I pitched my tent along the way, heading for a yoga ashram where I had stayed before. I identified a need to be around people, without necessarily engaging with them much of the time.

The routine involved rising around 5.00 a.m. and it was enlivening to feel the nature at that time of the day. I lived a short walk from the river, away from everyone else, and joined in with activities during the day. Often there was silence at meal times, and work involved attending to the forest or veggie garden during the day. It was a relaxing and very healing space. I also had my laptop if I felt like watching a movie at night for some western comforts to help me heal. One night I watched *P.S. I Love You*, and had a deep, therapeutic cry.

I continued travelling up the coast, attending different yoga weekends along the way, and meeting with many other people of the road. Everything was temporary, but we belonged to each other for those brief times, making meals together, as well as sharing in ceremonies and yogic practices. The gypsy in me was happy enough.

The further I travelled, the more opportunities presented. It was pleasant being free. I wasn't entirely sure what just happened to my life but, for now, my heart was dealing with it. Travel created healthy distractions and the possibilities of a new life.

At Chenrezig Buddhist Institute in the Eudlo mountains, I rented a simple room with a single bed. A reading lamp, window to the forest and shared bathroom, was everything I could ever need. By day I meditated, read, and walked in nature, and this supported sleeping well at night. The institute also had various teaching programs and meditations during the week, as well as guest lecturers and workshops on the weekends. They also had the best *Big Love Café,* in the middle of the grounds. At any time of the day, I could visit and enjoy coffee or tea, and the very best chocolate cake in the world. I don't recall another café where the kitchen staff was as happy so much of the time.

After six weeks or so, an inner prompting indicated that it was time for me to head home, to go back to family and friends with all the blessings I had received along the way. I headed for the coast and took my time driving South. I still needed the strong winds of the ocean beaches to blow away some more of the sadness that plagued my head, and my heart.

I visited my dear family in Melbourne, and then I managed to take sanctuary in Daylesford again.

Anew

I took guidance from the writings of Carl Jung: We are not what 'happens to us,' but 'what we choose to become.' Some days I felt like I had been thrown on a fire, and could do nothing except feel the pain. There I burned, as I learnt to let go of worldly attachments, and opened even more to spirit. What better process to help me to find the love I was seeking?

I recalled the meditation Ananda had run some years earlier, when she had asked us 'What does Love want of me?' I recalled my inner response, that love wanted everything. Clearly, I thought, this is what I needed to surrender to. My destiny was calling me, and my heart needed to open more.

The pain would often hit me hardest late at night, and I often struggled at these times. Usually the star- filled sky would help clear my mind and heart, and thankfully I had a dear friend I could call when it got too much, which it did on a couple of occasions. I was aware that what I experienced was just part of my path, and the intensity of the experience was something that I had to face and go through. It was pointless to make resistance, as this was how my soul and spirit were guiding me to the Grail.

A part of me has always sought to be all that I Am, and can be. At the end of the day, I needed to bear my own cross. I consoled myself that what happens in life is always perfect at some level of being. We are never victims unless we allow ourselves to think so. Every circumstance comes from previous choices or lessons that need to be learned. My journey was developing strengths that would support me in future times. The Jungian psychologist Robert A. Johnson suggested that if one is 'wishing for a true knight's task,' then 'take up the story inside yourself, where it lies unfinished, and proceed with it.'

My dear mentor gave me a practice that helped me to rebuild connection. Each night when I lay down to sleep, I called upon the Archangel Hope to fill my heart and help me to open again to life. I needed to remain mindful, and praying helped a lot.

Heartsong

While I was wondering what to do in life, my dear friend Lawrence was visiting from Denmark. As he sang about divine love, I felt my heart cry out 'Yes.' I knew immediately that I wanted to be part of this again. I found an old guitar and we began to play. A few weeks later, we were invited to create a concert at a local Healing Centre. Together with David from Bhakti days, the three of us offered an evening of heart songs. It felt like such a heavenly event, and was to be the beginning of a lot more music and my liberation from the shadow of grief.

Another dear friend and co-worker was headed for Europe, and invited me to be part of the journey. I purchased myself a new guitar, and travelled extensively for the next nine weeks. Through England, Scotland, the Republic of Ireland, Northern Ireland, Iceland and Denmark. Chandra ran workshops, and I got to assist. Everywhere we went, I sang sacred songs, which helped me to come alive again. Chandra was writing inspiring lyrics, and I found tunes to go with them. Our songwriting became quite prolific, and new songs kept coming for the work.

From a humble offering of three songs, in a concert in Australia before I left, I now played on several occasions with Lawrence in Denmark, as well as in workshops and lectures in England and Iceland. I also gave my own mini-concert in Ireland. It gave me so much hope to feel my connection to spirit in the music again.

It was an inspiring journey, visiting many historic and spiritually significant sites, and crossing so many lands. At times my heart felt heavy, occasionally when walking on quiet beaches, I still missed my beloved companion. I had left a part of my heart in Galway Bay the year before, and went back to pick it up again.

Soon after getting back to Australia, Lawrence was visiting again, and with David we formed a new band we called *Heartsong*. This was the beginning of many heartfelt and uplifting concerts. On occasions, another dear friend Per joined in, enlivening the work with his inspiring drumming.

I found awakening at these events, getting to express myself in music, humour and devotion. When I sang sacred songs, I felt free from all other concerns. Having the support of my closest friends, helped me to keep lifting, and opening to the next stage of my sacred journey.

On invitation from Lawrence, I returned to Scandinavia, and this became an elaborate concert tour. We travelled through Denmark from East to West, in Iceland from South to North, through Sweden into Norway, and around Ireland again. Making the decision to go to Scandinavia opened many doors for me, both earthly and spiritual. I also felt drawn to Barcelona, and followed my inner guidance to go there. The focus of my pilgrimage was to visit the grand cathedral *La Sagrada Familia* by Antonio Gaudi. I travelled nearly 17,000 kilometres to see one church, and I was not disappointed.

Denmark brought the great blessing of staying with Lawrence and another dear friend Gitte. The visit was like being a teenager again, and definitely one of the best times of my life. We had an easy living, fun sharing, heartfelt time in Helsingor, near the harbour, across the sound from Sweden. Life was pure joy.

In Ireland, at the Hill of Tara, when I was just about to share my first song, a voice of spirit spoke in my ear: 'Tonight you sing for the whole of Ireland.' Such was the nature of our blessed tour. We felt a constant support from the inner levels. There was a higher love overseeing our musical offerings. Everywhere we sang, we could see how people were lifted in spirit.

For three months, Lawrence and I played every venue that would have us, designing our concerts to offer a sacred space for each audience. We aimed that our music be relaxing and healing, dedicating our concerts to universal sister-brotherhood, and to love for all.

We concluded in Amsterdam, where I got to make my first album. With the help of Lawrence and dear Benjamin, we created something that I was very proud to offer the world: *Heartbeat*, a gift from my journey of the heart.

At the conclusion of all of these tours, I finally felt like I knew what to live for again. There were still challenges, but now I had the Light rekindled in my heart. I was again in contact with my soul nature and reason for being on the planet. I felt connection with something I truly loved: to sing, and to share that which is my heart.

My visits to Ireland introduced me to the writer William Butler Yeats. I enjoyed his writings and his reminder that the world 'is full of magic things, patiently waiting for our senses to grow sharper.' Many aspects of my life had brought me to this greater sensitivity and corresponding appreciation of life. Being on the road, I had visited many lands. I had made three trips to Europe in three years, and found myself travelling again to the heart of Australia, and up and down the east coast a couple of times. I also got to reconnect with my closest and most beloved friends. This was enough to finally bring me back to the joy of life.

After near constant travelling, I finally stopped in the peace of my Daylesford sanctuary, I allowed myself to do nothing for a while, reconnecting with a very valuable aspect of myself: my need to just be, and experience the subtlest of feelings.

I reconnected with the sacred feminine within myself, and now, I felt whole. The next morning I woke to the thought, 'I love life.' It was such a pleasant surprise. I stayed with the feeling as long as felt divine, and took it all in. Taking my time getting out of bed, I wanted to feel and savour the full truth of it:

'I love life!'

Final Reflections

Looking back at my life now, I see that once I had awakened to some degree, my path became one of following my heart. I chose freedom, and searched for love and truth. The option of taking an easier path was always there, but I had to be true to myself.

Over this journey I have learned about the effort involved in truly opening the petals of my heart, and responding to the call within me, to ever greater consciousness, service and joy.

I presently see how each of my lessons has even more subtle levels that I still need to open to, and I know that, given time, I will. I continue to find the truth in ancient wisdom, and ultimately, within my own being.

I have been fortunate indeed to have such a loving family, and to meet so many dear friends, lovers, mentors and teachers along the way. I have been so graced, to have people stand by me at times when I struggled the most.

Perhaps I have not always made the best choices, but I like to think that I have always learned from them. Ideally, each choice leads me deeper into comprehension of, and wakefulness in, the Divine. These days when I cry deeply, it is not so much from grief or sadness, but in gratitude to those who have helped me in opening my heart.

In search of an epiphany, I relax in the understanding that life is complex and vast, and that the experience will be both challenging as well as sublime. My main learning has been to appreciate its incredible gifts and share them with others.

I often wonder: what could be more important than to enjoy life and help each other along the way? It won't be too long before each of us returns to Essence, so best make the most of the opportunities now. Our world needs it, as much as it also enhances one's own experience.

In Theosophy, Alice Bailey suggests that goodwill is 'Man's first attempt to express the love of God,' and that 'its results on earth will be peace.' I like to think that this is true, and that more people will awaken to loving kindness as their practice. In the end, when we face how we have lived this life, the only question likely to be asked of us will be: 'Did you love?'

As I open to the Divine Grace the Light increases, and in working with what is given and what is revealed, I surrender to 'That' which calls me home. Back into Its Loving Heart. Towards the Lion.

In conclusion, taking a breath,
It is my hope that you find the Love that is seeking you,
And, in peace, I wish you well.

Love always,
Arjuna.

In loving memory of Tarajyoti Govinda (1958-1999)

'The journey towards wholeness can be a rich one. It involves accepting ourselves and allowing ourselves to be. It also demands a certain diligence and desire to better ourselves, not in terms of outer success, though that may come, rather, in terms of aspiration to live in Light, integration of our shadow and the manifestation of an inner peace which comes through living in truth and love.'

Tarajyoti Govinda
Becoming Whole: the psychology of light
www.devawings.com

Author

For over thirty years Arjuna has worked to understand the human condition and the inner life. He has travelled widely, creating healing music, facilitating sessions in dance as therapy, creative expression, and stress management. When not travelling, he treasures a simple life in the mineral springs town of Daylesford, Australia.

Arjuna's interests include heartfelt company, continual learning, sacred music, time in nature, community wellbeing, holistic psychology, eastern philosophy, cinema, world travel, gardening and Zen. He continues to enjoy and be fascinated by life.

Made in the USA
Charleston, SC
25 November 2015